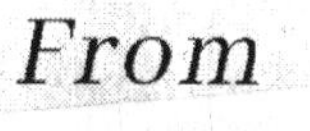

From

BERG [illegible] N

BR[illegible]KLYN

How a Holocaust survivor earned the protection of a Mafia boss.

Linda Rosenberg & Dr. Solomon Pinczewski

Table of Contents

FROM BERGEN-BELSEN TO BROOKLYN

A biography of Helsamenessen Pinczewski

A life story, a love story, a life affirming inspiration.

Linda Rosenberg & Dr. Solomon Pinczewski

PROLOGUE

DESPITE HER YEARS, HERBEHI declining health, and those who had sought to destroy her, my mother, Helen Pinczewski, triumphantly whirled around in the *Hora* circle. She accented each down beat of "*Hava Nagila*" until finally, out of breath, she sat down. Several old friends offered a toast, and I joined in the chorus of, "*Mazal tov!*" and "Happy fiftieth anniversary!" Then I raised my glass again. "To *Bubbe* Miriam, whose spirit continues to sustain us all."

My mother smiled broadly at me. "To my *Bubbe* Miriam," she echoed, "the burning coal that every day sparked my determination to survive. If not for her, I wouldn't be here today."

Although I never met my great grandmother—she died when my mother was just fifteen—I feel her presence at every significant moment in our lives. My mother believes Miriam's spirit is always with us, and I believe it, too.

As I leaned over to kiss my mother's steely gray head, a greeting card on the table caught my eye. "Happy Anniversary! You made it. Fifty Years!"

"Making it" to a Golden Anniversary had a unique meaning for my parents, whose first glimpse of each other had been in the striped uniforms of a Nazi work camp. Somehow, despite the bleak, humiliating nightmare of their existence in Zyberstoff, my mother and father found in their souls the yearning to reach out to each other. Incredibly, they retained enough of themselves to fall in love. My mother was just sixteen then, yet she was able to see past the terror and despair that surrounded her and respond to the vitality of David Pinczewski. Romantic poets write of love blossoming among the ruins. What of love that flowers amidst indignity, filth, and the daily horror of calculated dehumanization?

My mother never misses an opportunity to tell people about her first meeting with my father. "To tell the truth," she says with a mischievous twinkle, "he was a handsome boy, and right away I had an eye on him!" It is easy to believe my father had been good-looking. His squared-off-jaw and deep-set eyes retain traces of the smoldering good looks he had as a youth. My mother, too, is a beautiful woman. Her strong facial features and statuesque build give her presence that has not diminished with time.

I caught sight of Charles Drexler and dropped into the chair beside him. Charles's mother, who had been very close with mine throughout the war and post-war years, had died when he was fourteen. Since then, my mother had treated him like one of her own. We exchanged the usual pleasantries, and he regaled me with the latest antics of those who choose to teach and study at Berkeley. Then, with a shift in tone, he said, "You know, I think this is the happiest day of my life." Without a moment's hesitation, I agreed with him. He looked across at my mother. Her eyes met his, and she waved and blew him a kiss. He smiled fondly at her. "I don't know," he said, shaking his head. "How does she manage to be so upbeat? After what she's been through?"

"I use that phrase all the time," I said, "*after what she's been through,* but the truth is I don't have a clue what it really means. I don't know what she went through." Charles raised his eyebrows and cocked his head to the side the way he did when something caught his interest.

"Some of it, I know. She has this repertoire of reminiscences about her life in Europe before the war. Some anecdotes about the Holocaust and what happened after it. Stuff she's talked about so much it doesn't hurt anymore. But they're all rough sketches. No details really." I paused and then added rather lamely, "I should know more."

Charles stared at me and blinked a few times. His Adam's apple bobbed up in his neck, and, although he said nothing, I could guess what he was thinking. And he was right. Although I regularly planned to bring up the subject, I always found reasons to put off the conversation for a better time. If we were together for a celebration, I didn't want to spoil the mood. If it was a sad time, I didn't want to make things worse. The truth was that I was afraid. How would I react to the horrors of daily life in Bergen-Belsen?

Suddenly, I was struck with an acute awareness of dwindling opportunities. How many more times would there be? With a new sense of urgency, I realized I had never confronted the possibility that time could just run out on me. All at once, it became absolutely clear to me that there was no time to lose.

The next time I saw my parents, I put a small tape recorder, a yellow legal pad, and two sharp pencils on the table between the china teacups and the homemade *babke* of which my mother was so justly proud. "I'm going to write your life story," I told them. "Every time I visit you're going to tell me about things you remember and I'm going to put it in a book."

My father looked uncomfortable. "What's to tell?" he asked with a shrug. "We told it all already. Maybe your mother—"

"Are you kidding," she interrupted him, "we told nothing. Even to the Spielberg interviewer we couldn't tell it all. Who could say such things on television? Sol, if you want stories, I'll tell you stories. Plenty of stories, and not only how we suffered. I'll tell you some stories from the candy store that will make you laugh so much you'll wet your pants."

"He doesn't want to know about the candy store," my dad's voice was thick with some emotion I could not identify. "He wants to know about the camps. Suddenly everyone wants to know about the camps."

"Forget about it! What do you mean everyone wants to know? A couple of people maybe. One or two ask you about it because they saw *Schindler's List.* But what happens when you start to tell them? Suddenly they have an appointment. What do I care? My Sol wants to know."

"That's what I said," grumbled my father. "He wants to know about the camps. Not the candy store."

“Mom. Dad. Don’t start arguing now. I want to know it all, starting with Poland, and your parents, and *Bubbe* Miriam. I have fond memories of the candy store too.”

As always, *Bubbe* Miriam’s name had a soothing effect. “*Bubbe* Miriam, she was something,” said my mother, and my father nodded in agreement.

He stood up and walked over to the mantelpiece. From the mass of discordantly framed photographs falling over each other, he took the faded picture of my mother’s grandmother, Miriam. My great-uncle David had given her the photograph soon after we arrived in New York, and she loved to relate how I responded when she showed it to me.

“She doesn’t look like a dead person,” I had said.

“That’s because she is still alive... inside here”—she touched her chest—“and inside there.” She touched mine. My mother gave me a big hug for that response and thanked God for giving her a boy who understood what was what.

The picture had been taken in the front yard of Miriam’s home in the Polish town of Sosnowiec. Standing straight-backed, her feet firmly planted on the cobbled pathway that led to her front door, she looked as permanent and solid as an ancient sequoia tree. She was smiling a little self-consciously at the photographer, but her eyes were undaunted and clear. As I now studied the photograph with renewed interest, I imagined I saw her returning my gaze in a way that suggested she approved of my decision to write her granddaughter's life story.

Each time I asked my mother to talk with me about her life, she began with an amusing story about the candy store they had owned in Brooklyn in the early fifties. She is a wonderful storyteller, and I laughed as hard as she promised I would, but not nearly as hard as she did. Then, when she felt we had laughed enough, she would tell me how they suffered in those early years. How poor we were, how hard she and my father worked, and how difficult things were for me. I told her I remembered some of it, and she would hug me and cry a little. Then she would make tea.

One morning, I went over to visit and discovered she had fallen in the shower. A friend had taken her to the doctor, who diagnosed a broken wrist and put her left arm in a cast.

"It's unbelievable!" she said when I asked what had happened. "I fell and I didn't get hurt. Just this arm. Oy, I'm so lucky. Do you know how easy it is to break a hip at my age?"

"Yes, I do know that. What I don't know is how you always find the bright side of everything."

"You gotta look for it."

I shrugged.

"Listen, Sol," she went on, "you know what happened to me with the eyes. When I was a baby they put in bad eye drops, and I was blind for three years. Do you think that because I couldn't see the sun it wasn't shining? You gotta remember that the good stuff is there even when you can't see it. To be honest with you, it's not easy, but you gotta try."

Eventually she told me about the camps, all of it, including the things she couldn't say on television. But that was later. In the beginning there was the small Polish town of Sosnowiec.

CHAPTER ONE

HELEN GLEITMAN WAS BORN on June 17, 1924, in Sosnowiec, a small city in southwestern Poland. At that time, the three million Jews of the Polish republic comprised the second largest Jewish community in the world. Poland was a cultural and literary center of Ashkenazi life. It was a hothouse for imaginative Yiddish writers, fervent Zionists, and devout Hasidic leaders.

Unlike the Jews in Western Europe, Polish Jews were totally excluded from the non-Jewish community and with less opportunity to assimilate, were under no pressure to adopt the norms of the surrounding society. There was no attempt to tone down the expressions of Jewish traditions in order to make them more socially acceptable. On the contrary, the Jews of Poland celebrated their uniqueness. The Jewish holidays were scrupulously observed. On Pesach, the story of the Jewish liberation from Pharaoh's tyranny was told with great energy and verve. Not one detail was omitted from the tale. The young children nodded off to sleep at the table long before they tasted the chicken soup and gefilte fish. This wasn't a problem because their mothers had all surreptitiously given them dinner before the *seder*. So now they were simply covered up and made comfortable in their chairs. After the meal, every verse of "Chad Gad Yaw" was sung, and the repetitions of "*Dayenu*" were accompanied by pounding on the table as the voices became more and more hoarse.

Yet the Polish Jews never forgot that they were at best tolerated, and more often despised, by their non-Jewish neighbors. The *Pesach matzo* was purchased secretly at night because many Poles believed the medieval superstition that matzo was baked with the blood of Christian children. The custom of leaving a door ajar so that the spirit of the prophet Elijah could attend the Seder was regretfully abandoned, as it was considered great sport to send a donkey or even a pig through the open doors of Jewish homes. The Jews of Sosnowiec made these adjustments as they were needed and continued to revere their God and practice their traditions.

The Sabbath was their most sacred day. Preparations began on Friday afternoon with the kneading and baking of the *challah,* and the plucking of a freshly killed chicken. In the evening, *Shabbat* candles were lit, and the men walked to services at the neighborhood synagogue. The pious observance of *Shabbat* gave the Jews of Sosnowiec a sense of control over their lives, and some sanctuary from the stress of their daily lives. The Gleitman family welcomed *Shabbat* with joy each Friday at sunset, and the day of rest and prayer that followed was peaceful and rejuvenating for them all.

Benjamin Gleitman worked as a kosher butcher in the slaughterhouse and made a good living. He'd learned five languages during his seven years in the Polish army, which included seeing active service in the First World War. He often entertained Helen by repeating a sentence in every language he knew. His wife, Leah, was not amused by Benjamin's silliness. She did not indulge in frivolous behavior, but she did make sure that her family was fed and clothed as well as any family on the street.

Helen enjoyed her childhood. It was filled with security and love at home and camaraderie and fun at school. If she got into an inordinate number of fights, it didn't bother anyone but her mother. Helen had been blinded shortly after her birth, and when her sight was restored she had to wear heavy protective dark glasses for many years. This condition, together with her unruly red hair, caused her to be taunted mercilessly by the Christian children who considered all Jewish children fair game, anyway. Leah encouraged her to ignore her tormentors, but that was not Helen's way. When a boy in the park called her a "kretinye" (fool), she tripped him and he fell into a puddle, ruining his Sunday clothes. When the girls taunted her saying, "Go back to Palestine, ugly Jew girl," Helen grabbed the leader's hair and pulled until she cried.

But even Helen knew that during the weeks leading up to the Christian holidays of Christmas and Easter, all Jewish children had to give the Christian children a wide berth. Incited by anti-Semitic priests and emboldened by alcohol, adults often joined their children in hurling racial slurs across the park, and fathers encouraged their sons to beat up Jewish boys.

Included in the treaty that ended World War I and established the Polish republic were provisions guaranteeing civil and political equality to national minorities. Specifically, minorities were given the right to establish their own religious and political institutions.

In Sosnowiec, there existed a parallel system of Jewish and Polish public schools, and Helen was legally entitled to be educated in either of these systems. The Jewish school was located just across the street in the basement of a residential apartment building. Although it was not as spacious and modern as the Polish school, the education was equally good, and Benjamin knew she would be safer and more welcome there. Her friend Hela Piotkowski, who lived in an apartment above the school, and the Zaks children who lived next door also went to the Jewish school.

In the evenings, Benjamin taught Helen to play his guitar. Cousin Feivel played the mandolin, and their repertoire included Yiddish, Polish, and Russian songs. Helen, who had a sweet, strong voice and a true ear, often brought home the most recent hits. "Pani Maryska Telefonitska" (Mary and the Telephone Operator) was the most popular with the neighbors and it usually brought them out into the street to listen to the lively music.

As much as she loved her father and enjoyed her friends, Helen's closest bond was with her paternal grandmother, *Bubbe* Miriam. For a woman of her time and place, Miriam had an extraordinarily sophisticated understanding of the world. She was well read, had a quick perceptive mind, and believed that the Creator was a lot more flexible than they gave

Him credit for. In deference to her studious, more orthodox, husband, *Bubbe* Miriam kept her opinions to herself. She never revealed the breadth of her knowledge of the world or the depth of her wisdom. As her community expected, she focused on being a devoted wife and mother, keeping her scarf on her head and her rolled up shirt-sleeves below the elbows.

She had resigned herself to talking only to God about her views of His world, until, when Helen was about six years old, she recognized in her grandchild a kindred spirit. Helen soon discovered that while her questions elicited just a word or two from her mother, *Bubbe* Miriam turned every query into a fascinating discussion.

Also, Miriam was sure that God in His Wisdom would understand if His rules were occasionally bent a little, so Helen knew that if she went to her grandmother's house on Saturday, after services at the synagogue on Dekert Street, she might find that *Bubbe* Miriam had left twenty-five groshen on a corner table—the exact cost of a movie ticket.

Then, because it was against the laws of the Sabbath to handle money on a Saturday, *Bubbe* Miriam would clear it with God, telling Him that if He needed to punish someone for this transgression, it should be her, Miriam. Let the young child enjoy herself.

Bubbe Miriam saw life as a valuable gift. She believed every precious moment of it should be celebrated. Pain, loss, and sadness had to be felt. Loved ones who were lost had to be mourned. However, in between, every good day had to be appreciated and enjoyed. She didn't just advocate her world view, she acted on it. When one afternoon she saw Helen sitting by herself at the side of the frozen lake watching her friends skate, she went to confront her son, Benjamin.

She found him at home, oiling the front door. "Benjamin, come inside and sit down," she said with no preamble, "I need to talk to you."

Benjamin put down the oil and the rag and complied with her request. "And 'Hello' to you too, Mama," he said good-naturedly.

"Now listen to me," she said, pointing a parental finger at him. "You are forgetting something very important. Children need to play and have fun, doing what the other children do."

"Mama, what are you talking about?"

"Sliding shoes. I'm talking about sliding shoes," said Miriam, making up a compound because she did not know the word for ice-skates. Without giving

Benjamin a chance to speak, she went on, "I know you are afraid Helen will get hurt on the ice, but that is up to God, not up to you. From you I want permission to buy her sliding shoes. My cousin has them in his store. I can get them for her today. Tomorrow she can be happily circling the ice and not sitting like a stone on a bench."

Leah, who had come in for the latter part of Miriam's tirade, was dead-set against allowing Helen to risk breaking a leg on the ice. She scowled at the love shining from her husband's eyes as he listened to his mother, and she knew he would not disagree with her. That very day, Miriam, always as good as her word, bought the skates.

Helen soon became proficient at ice-skating. Each time she came off the ice smiling and exhilarated by the brisk winter air, she thanked *Bubbe* Miriam for the skates and thanked God for *Bubbe* Miriam.

At this time, one out of three Polish Jews was dependent on Jewish welfare organizations. In the Gleitman's neighborhood, there lived a family with seven children, none of whom ever went to bed with a full stomach. Each Saturday, Helen and her friend, Mania, collected all the food that was left over from the Sabbath meals and took it to the dismal cellar apartment where the hungry children eagerly awaited them.

Being an only child, Helen enjoyed the tumult. She loved the affection she received from the children, especially the hugs from arms of the youngest toddler who delighted in grabbing fistfuls of her enticing red hair.

One Saturday, Helen and Mania were met by the child's weeping mother. Between sobs she told the girls that the baby had contracted typhus and had died the night before. Shortly after that, Helen came down with typhus, too. She developed pneumonia and diphtheria as complications, and, in accordance with the medical practice of the time, she was quarantined in her bedroom. She showed no signs of recovery, despite three months of isolation and protection from the dangers of fresh air, so the local doctor gave Benjamin the name and address of a Jewish specialist he knew in England. At home Benjamin wrote to him at once, stayed patiently at home for two weeks, and then went each day to the Post Office, anxiously awaiting an answer and medicine from the doctor.

Throughout this frightening and lonely ordeal, *Bubbe* Miriam kept up Helen's morale. Although she was forbidden to go into the sick room, she spoke with Helen through the window, assuring her granddaughter that she would be well again soon. She described the changing seasons outside her room, and she made her laugh at the antics of the children on the street. In order to encourage Helen to eat, she described the delicious smells coming from the bakery and cooked her favorite dish, *lokshen* pudding packed with raisins and cinnamon. She talked about what fun Helen would soon have, going to movies and practicing turns on her sliding shoes. Helen chuckled weakly at her grandmother's stories, tried to eat her food, and said repeatedly, "Don't worry so much, Bubbe."

When she wasn't talking to Helen, Miriam looked up at the clear winter sky and talked to God. She pleaded with Him to spare her granddaughter's life, reminding the creator that Helen had already suffered three years of blindness and that she was an only child. "Take me and leave this child!" entreated *Bubbe* Miriam. "She still has her whole life to live."

Because she knew God had many other things to take care of, *Bubbe* Miriam also went to see the Radomska *Rebbe*, whom she had known since he was a smooth-faced yeshiva. student.

"Miriam," he said, as they sat in his office sipping hot black tea, "I have a suggestion. It is rather unusual for our modern times, but maybe in this case..."

"Tell me, *Rebbe*, please," said Miriam.

"Very well, but listen carefully and do not interrupt, although you will want to."

"I won't say a word until you tell me to."

"You must cut off the head of a young, healthy chicken."

"Wha—"

"You promised not to interrupt. The head must then be put into a small sack, and your granddaughter must keep it with her at all times. For the next year, she must never go anywhere without it, even after she has recovered and has gone back to school."

Miriam could not control her incredulity. "*Rebbe*, are you serious?"

The *Rebbe*'s eyes lit up with surprise. Only Miriam would so blatantly question his advice. He found it refreshing and enjoyed the moment. "Yes, I am serious. Miriam," he said as his eyes twinkled at her, "there are still many things in this world that you and I don't understand. I have heard that this has helped other children, and I believe we should try it."

Miriam sipped her tea thoughtfully. He was certainly right about how much she did not understand, and the *Rebbe* was after all a highly respected spiritual leader. Who was she to disagree with him?

"Very well, *Rebbe*," she said. "Thank you, and may you and your family be well."

The chicken was slaughtered and medicines arrived from England. Over the next few weeks, Helen regained her strength. By spring, she was able to leave her bedroom and go back to school. Since the family was not certain whether it was their prayers, the medicine, or the chicken's head that had affected the recovery, they felt compelled to follow the Rabbi's instructions. Helen put the sack with the chicken's head into her pocket book and, hiding it under her coat, reluctantly carried it to school each day. However, as the days became warmer, it began to smell, and Helen became the laughing stock of her schoolmates.

Bubbe Miriam paid a second visit to the *Rebbe*. She thanked him for his help and then explained that in this imperfect world a young girl could not walk around carrying the head of a chicken. He understood and exchanged the chicken head for a monetary coin over which he said a blessing. He also gave her a second name, "Alta," which means "old." From then on, her name would be "Old Helen"—*Alta Chaya* in Yiddish—in the hope that this would turn out to be a prediction, and the new name would confuse the Angel of Death.

CHAPTER TWO

IN SEPTEMBER OF 1933, Adolf Hitler became Chancellor of Germany. His brown shirted gang of fascist thugs had nothing but disdain for the advances of German civilization and introduced a brutal dictatorship. The Nazis made no attempt to hide their hatred of Jews; on the contrary, they proclaimed it. In his public speeches, Hitler went so far as to state the salvation of the German people lay in eliminating Jews from all of Europe.

In Poland, too, anti-Semitism began to increase. Hitler's success had shown Polish nationalists that the Nazi approach of scapegoating Jews could make a small group of extremists very powerful. In 1935, Marshall Joseph Pilsudski, the head of the Polish republic, died, and the nationalists seized their opportunity. A military junta with fascist undertones took power in Poland, and, inspired by the Nazi's program of organized anti-Semitism, it disregarded the Republic's constitution and abandoned all guarantees of civil and political rights for Jews.

All of Poland, from the Jews who shuddered in trepidation, to the militant nationalists who quivered with glee, watched as Hitler began planning for a thousand year Reich. The Nazis attempted to legitimize their reign of terror by enacting the anti-Semitic Nuremberg Laws. These laws officially categorized Jews as belonging to an inferior race and forced them to identify themselves by sewing a yellow star onto their outer clothing. Social, religious, and economic restrictions were placed on Jewish life. Jewish businesses were boycotted and later taken over by non-Jewish Germans. In Hitler's vernacular, they were Aryanized. Jewish doctors and lawyers were barred from practice.

In Sosnowiec, Benjamin and his family gathered around the kitchen table each evening to read the newspapers. With mounting horror, they read accounts of the anti-Semitic fervor that seemed to be engulfing the German people. Theodore Lewald was forced to resign as President of the German Olympic Committee merely because one of his grandparents was Jewish. People were flocking to huge nighttime rallies where the paintings of Marc Chagall, the writings of Sigmund Freud, and the poetry of

Heinrich Heine were thrown into a bonfire and burned to cinders.

Miriam soon realized that Hitler was the most formidable enemy her people had ever confronted. She took very seriously his threats to eliminate all the Jews of Europe, and she understood that the increasing anti-Semitism in Poland indicated clearly that Poland would provide no refuge for Jews in the face of Hitler's dangerous designs. She already had two sons living in America, and she urged Benjamin to join his brothers in New York. In vain, she tried to enlist Leah's support for this plan, but Leah was adamant that there was no need for such drastic action.

"Anti-Semitism in Poland! So what's new?" she demanded. "Sometimes things are better, sometimes they're worse. Nu? As for Hitler, what do we care about him? Hitler is in Germany. Let the Germans worry about Hitler."

The newspapers reported on Hitler's expansionist plans and Germany's uncontested annexation of Austria and the Sudetenland. In spite of these developments, Leah remained intransigent, unable to see Benjamin's departure as anything but an abandonment of herself and their child.

On November 10th, 1938, Benjamin came home later than usual, pale faced and trembling. He could barely speak as he handed his cousin Feivel the newspaper. "Please, read this aloud," he said. "Since my eyes refuse to understand the meaning of these words, let me see if my ears will take it in."

For the first time ever, silence filled every nook and cranny of the room. Even the pot bubbling on the stove became quiet. Feivel cleared his throat. He began reading. Then stopped. His eyes jumped ahead, and his knees crumpled under the weight of the words that he could not speak.

Finally, it was Miriam who read the article aloud.

In what was later to become known as the Night of the Broken Glass, or Kristallnacht, 190 German synagogues and 7,000 Jewish businesses were destroyed. Violence that broke all the usual laws and yet seemed governed by indefinable laws of its own, killed 100 Jews and imprisoned 20,000 others.

Leah tried to minimize the horror. To put it into a familiar context. "It's a pogrom. A terrible pogrom, but still a pogrom." Her words were met with the silence of unbearable truth as each person tried and failed to take comfort from her words.

The next day Miriam took Benjamin aside and ardently pleaded with him. "*Tatenu,*" she said, taking his hands in hers. "Please, you must listen to me. What is happening now is like nothing we have ever known before. You must leave. Go to America."

"Mama, I can't do it. Who will take care of you and Leah and Helen? I cannot leave you with no protection."

"My son, listen to me. You have a strong arm and a strong heart, but you cannot protect us from this devil. You must go to America. David and Sam are there. They will help you to get papers for us, and then you will send for us and we will come too. In the meantime, I will take care of Leah and Helen. Please, Benjamin, at least get a passport."

Benjamin agreed to do that.

One evening, to everyone's surprise, they were joined at the kitchen table by a young friend of Benjamin's, David Weichman. David was a timid young bachelor who had inherited his father's bakery. He should have been there, baking the bread for the next day.

He slumped into a chair. "I turned off the ovens," he said. "For seventy years Weichmans never turned the ovens off except on Pesach and Yom Kippur. But after they made us put our names on the door of our businesses, fewer and fewer people came to the shop—they went to the bakers with Christian names.

I didn't mind. I was still making a living, and at the end of the day I donated loaves to the poor families in the neighborhood. But then students began threatening my customers more and more and today, I only sold six loaves." He sighed. So, "I have come to say goodbye. I have received my papers and I am going to America. When I am settled I will send for my mother and sister." He hesitated as if unsure if he should continue, then added, "Benjamin, excuse me for telling you what to do, but you should come, too. It's all over for us here." Benjamin looked across at Leah, who turned on her heel and left the room, muttering under her breath about men who left their women alone in these uncertain times.

Two weeks later, in the spring of 1939, when Polish Prime Minister Slawoj-Skladowski gave his backing to the economic war against Polish Jewry, Benjamin finally had a passport photo taken, a small black and white of his head and shoulders.

But he never got to use it.

On September 1, 1939, Germany invaded Poland. The German air force overwhelmed the outnumbered and poorly equipped Polish forces. By September 4th, German troops occupied Sosnowiec.

From the moment the soldiers arrived, Helen's life changed irrevocably. Uncertainty and fear replaced stability. The security and protection she had come to rely upon disappeared overnight. Before she was fully awake on that first morning, the Zaks children from next door, Tolla, Mania, Chesa, and little Rose came running in to say goodbye. Their parents had packed all their belongings into a wagon and were going to hide out in a small neighboring village until the German occupation was over.

Romek, the oldest son, refused to go with them. He was stubborn, strong-willed, and proud, and, although Benjamin usually valued these traits, he realized they were dangerous qualities in uncertain times. He went over to the electrical appliance store on Chachaji Maya Street where Romek worked and beckoned to him through the window. Reluctantly, the seventeen-year-old boy came out to talk to him.

"Romek, your mother asked me to speak with you," he began.

Romek interrupted him at once. "Mr. Gleitman, with due respect, I have made up my mind. This is my family's home. My father earned the money to pay for it; my mother scrubbed it and kept it clean. We have celebrated *Shabbat* under its roof every week since I was born. I am not leaving. When the Germans come they will find me in my house where I belong."

Benjamin looked at Romek's glittering defiant eyes and he knew the boy would not be persuaded. "I respect your decision," he said. "May God be with you."

Proud and defiant, Romek Zaks was the first casualty of the German occupation of Sosnowiec. That evening, as soldiers triumphantly paraded up the street where the Zaks family lived, one of them laughed and shouted, "The Jews are hiding inside their hutches like scared rabbits."

Romek defiantly sauntered out to the railing of his porch. Nonchalantly, he leaned against the wall and looked directly at the soldier who had spoken. The soldier simply opened fire and shot Romek where he stood, killing him instantly. Twelve other Jews were murdered in Sosnowiec that day.

In the meantime, after just one day of travelling along the back roads, the Zaks family realized that they had underrated the thoroughness of the German war machine. There were soldiers everywhere. No village was too inconsequential for the SS. They spent the night with friends and early the next morning they returned home. Helen was the first one to see the wagon returning. She ran inside to where her father was helping to prepare Romek for burial.

"Papa, they're back," she yelled.

"Who? The soldiers?"

"No. Tolla and Mania. I saw the wagon."

"Where?" Benjamin took her hand. "Show me. Which way?"

"There, Papa."

Benjamin ran up the street and waved his friends to a stop. Helen watched as he climbed up onto the seat, but when Romek's father stood up on the wagon and screamed to the heavens, "No! No! Not my Romek," she burst into tears and ran to get *Bubbe* Miriam.

Bubbe would know what to do.

Later that day, they buried Romek. Helen waited for her father or grandmother to say something to make it better. But they didn't. They stood so still, so silent, and so pale at the grave, that Helen felt utterly alone for the first time in her life. In the pit of her stomach she felt that something deep inside the world was broken, and that no one could fix it.

She became even more convinced that the world as she knew it had ended when, on the following Saturday, for the first time ever, Benjamin did not take her to the synagogue.

One look at his face, and she knew not to ask him why they were not going.

Benjamin wrapped his head and shoulders into his flimsy blue and white prayer shawl, clutching it to himself as if it was a winter coat protecting him from a blizzard. One by one other men she recognized came to the house and huddled around her dad, talking in whispers until they had a *minyan;* the minimum number of ten men required by Jewish law for the recitation of *Kaddish*—simultaneously a prayer for the dead and praise for God. Helen helped her mother make tea. But no-one stayed long enough to drink it. It was very late when Benjamin returned home.

It was late the next day when Benjamin returned home. His hands were blackened with soot. He wheezed and coughed as he explained that the Dekert Street Synagogue had been burned to the ground in the early hours of that morning. He had spent the day searching through the ashes, retrieving prayer books, torah scrolls, and other sacred artifacts.

A curfew was strictly enforced. Any Jews found on the street after six at night would be arrested and summarily shot. Every man, woman, and child was forced to wear a white armband with the yellow star. "Special Day" decrees were issued regularly. One day was declared gold day, and everybody had to bring their gold to a central collection point. On another day it was silver or fur. If a German soldier noticed a bedroom set or some other piece of furniture he liked in a Jewish house, he just put a ticket on it, and the next day a truck came by to take it away.

Young Jewish men were regularly rounded up to build roads and railways, drain swamps, and provide labor for factories. Only Jews who could show that they were providing essential services for the German war effort at home could avoid being transported to labor camps. There were a few German-owned workshops in the area around Sosnowiec, and because jobs there were in great demand the situation provided fertile ground for corruption.

SS Chief Richard Heydrich had ordered his advance troops, the Einsatzgruppen, to establish a committee of Jewish leaders in each Jewish community they subjugated. The real purpose of these local councils was to manipulate the Jews into organizing their own destruction, although ostensibly they were to take a census to ensure that everyone received housing and food. The formation of these *Judenrats* aroused deep misgivings in Jews throughout Poland and created imponderable dilemmas. Some believed that the community needed some intermediary to negotiate on their behalf, much as the Court Jew had done with the Polish king during the Middle Ages. Others realized at once that the Judenrat would have to obey all instructions of the SS and thus have neither autonomy nor options. They would merely be an instrument of German oppression.

A few unscrupulous individuals took advantage of this situation. Among them were Jacob Gens in Vilna, Mordechai Chaim Rumkowski in Lodz, and Moses Merin in Sosnowiec.

When a Central Committee of Jewish Councils of Elders for East Upper Silesia—The Centrala, was established, Moses Merin, a ruthless little man with vaulting ambition, manipulated his way to the top. Merin now controlled 37 Jewish councils and a Jewish population of over 100,000. He compared himself to his biblical namesake, Moses, and believed he had been chosen by God to play a special role in deciding which Jewish people would be delivered from these oppressors. He developed direct contacts with German administrators throughout the Third Reich, and soon he was able to travel freely, not only in Occupied Poland, but also in Austria, Czechoslovakia, and Nazi Germany. He met with the leaders of the Judenrat of Warsaw and Lodz in an attempt to extend his authority over all of Polish

Jewry. He even met with Adolf Eichmann in Berlin to discuss the mass emigration of Poland's Jews. He also controlled the sale of *sounders,* life-saving tickets to work in local German factories instead of being deported.

Despite all this, Miriam never reproached her son for not taking steps to emigrate while he could. Not even in her heart in the middle of the night did she blame him for his lack of courage and foresight, for she knew he had acted out of love for her, his wife, and his daughter, and she could not blame him for that. But now she wished Benjamin and his friend Shmuel would not continue working in the slaughterhouse since the ritual slaughtering of animals according to Jewish dietary laws was declared illegal and punishable by death.

Benjamin insisted that his community should have access to kosher meat, but he had learned a hard lesson. His eyes were now wide-open to what was going on around him, and they only worked at night. He also knew that it was only a matter of time before young women would also be forced to labor for the Reich, and that meant Helen was in danger. The Judenrat had given the SS the names and addresses of all the inhabitants of Sosnowiec. When they wanted his daughter, the SS would know exactly where to find her. Benjamin wrestled with the problem. He knew the deportations were always meticulously planned well in advance of the *aktion*, and so the resistance groups could usually give the community a few hours warning. Benjamin felt sure he would have time to get Helen out of sight. The question was where could she hide? Each time he thought about this, Benjamin came up with the same name, Yanek. He would ask his Polish neighbor, Yanek, for help. He and Yanek had always gotten along well, and he knew that Yanek was deeply disturbed by what was happening in their town. Yanek was a peace-loving, religious man who just wanted to be left alone to run his farm. He and Benjamin talked about their troubles. Yanek appreciated that Benjamin understood that it was hard enough to make a living as a farmer in good times, but now that the German soldiers helped themselves to anything they wanted, it was almost impossible.

The evening Benjamin went across the street to speak with Yanek, he was too anxious to make small talk and so he came straight to the point. He explained that Helen needed a place to hide from the Germans.

"Of course. Whenever you think she is not safe at home send her to us. They must not get their hands on your lovely Helen. They have taken more than enough from us."

Benjamin let out the breath he had been holding all day. Yanek patted his friend's shoulder. "What did you think I would say? I have children of my own. I know you would do the same for me. Sit down and let's have a drink." He picked up a clear glass bottle. "Let's drink to our big-mouthed leaders who said we would surrender nothing to Hitler, not even the buttons off our uniforms? In one day we surrendered it all, the whole country." He filled two glasses with a white smoky liquid. "I'm not sure exactly what this is made of, but it does warm the belly."

Benjamin had friends in Bedzin where the resistance movement had links with Warsaw, and he was one of the first to hear the rumor that girls between fourteen and sixteen years old would be picked up in the next deportation. Yanek assured him that Helen would be safe in his house for as long as she needed to hide. Each day they listened for the rumble of trucks in the distance and less than a week later that sound had Helen running across the road to Yanek's house.

"My father told me to come here. The Germans are coming."

"When?" Yanek stepped outside with her.

"Now. We heard the trucks."

"But… you can't come inside." Helen sensed the fear in this adult who was supposed to take care of her and became very frightened herself.

"We… we're not ready. Run to the barn. Go up the ladder and hide under the straw. Don't breathe, don't move, don't sneeze, until I come to get you. Go quickly now, and remember, be very quiet."

She obeyed and pulled the heavy door closed behind her. She climbed the ladder, crawled up into a haystack, and covered herself with hay. She immediately felt a tickle in her nose. "Don't sneeze!" Yanek had said. "Don't sneeze."

CHAPTER THREE

A SHORT WHILE LATER, four SS soldiers arrived at the Gleitman house looking for the young, healthy Jewess who was registered as living there. Leah answered their heavy pounding on the door. The shortest and stockiest of the four stepped forward and demanded to see Helen.

"She is no longer living here," said Leah, her voice trembling as she repeated the words Benjamin had instructed her to say. "She was taken to work in a factory."

"Don't lie to me. I have her name right here. She will be returned to you when her work is done. Right now the Fuhrer needs her."

Leah swallowed hard. "You have taken her already," she said, weeping into her apron. "She is gone." Her tears were real, but her crying merely annoyed the SS men, who had long ago become deaf to a mother's sobs. They pushed past her into the house and went from room to room in search of

Helen. When they didn't find her, they stormed out swearing and shouting that resistance was futile. They would not stop searching until they had her. They made their way methodically up the street, brutalizing family members in their frustration, as it became clear that the Jews had received some advance warning and their search for the missing Jewesses continued to be almost fruitless.

From her hiding place in Yanek's barn, Helen could hear them coming. She wriggled more deeply into the haystack so her head and arms were fully covered. What would Yanek do if they came to his door? He didn't seem like a very brave man. Faced with the trucks, the uniforms, and the guns would he continue to protect her? She knew of people who had been turned over to the Germans for no more than a bar of chocolate or a bottle of vodka. She felt dizzy and was afraid she would faint, but a second gunshot nearby made her jump. Her mouth filled with straw as she gasped with fright.

She was still spitting the straw out of her dry mouth when Yanek rushed into the barn, grabbed one of her legs, and whispered, "Get down. You must go. I'm sorry. They're searching every house. If they find you, we will all be killed!" He pulled her down and hustled her out of the back door of the barn. "Go quickly. Run. I'm sorry. Tell your father I'm sorry."

Taking great care not to be seen, she crept around the back of the barn, crouched there, and watched the soldiers go into the house. As soon as the door closed behind them she sprinted down the street staying close to the buildings, and undetected made her way to the one place she felt safe.

She found *Bubbe* Miriam standing at the door of her house looking out at the horror unfolding before her in the streets. Helen approached so quietly her grandmother didn't see her until she appeared on the doorstep, looking like a tattered scarecrow.

"Bubbe..." Helen began, with a sob.

"No. No crying yet, *Maminu,*" said Miriam, immediately taking in the situation. "They haven't been here yet. Quick, in my bed. Lie very still."

Helen climbed into the bed, and Miriam covered her with two thick heavy comforters. Then Miriam prepared herself. She untied the neat bun so that her hair hung in scraggly knots across her face. She draped a thick shawl haphazardly around her shoulders, and sat staring into space at the open door.

When the soldiers barged in, she smiled distractedly at them. "Oh my, you boys look frozen," she said. "Why don't you come in? Come in and I'll make you some hot tea." Pretending to be lame as well as senile, she wrapped the shawl more tightly around her and hobbled back a few steps to let them in.

The soldiers looked questioningly at her, and at each other. The lady was obviously harmless. The tea was tempting, but they had work to do. "Danke Schoen," they said politely, "but we cannot stop."

Miriam nodded and smiled, keeping her face expressionless. She sat down again. She had gambled that they would consider her invitation to come in as proof that she had nothing to hide. However, she knew things could have taken a very different turn, and they might be back. It was not over yet. For the rest of the day, Miriam sat in her chair muttering to herself with the door half open, and Helen lay unmoving under the covers. Only when the last soldier and the last truck had left did Miriam finally fall exhausted into the bed next to her.

The next morning Benjamin came up with a new plan. He would build a hiding place for Helen inside the house. That way they would not have to depend on anyone else for help. Benjamin knocked out a part of the wall behind the wooden closet in his bedroom, and there he made a bunker for Helen. The small space made her claustrophobic and panicked. Her arms and legs seemed too long to be folded into the hole. They squashed her in, but when they pushed the closet into place in front of her she screamed to be let out. "Don't worry. I can get used to it. I'll try again tomorrow," she promised.

And she did. She not only tried, she succeeded. She had no choice. An SS truck pulled up outside her house without warning. Leah, hearing the screech of tires, looked out the window and screamed, "It's them!" Helen, too terrified to be claustrophobic, immediately curled herself into the dark bunker behind the heavy closet.

However, this time the soldiers had not come looking for Helen. It was Benjamin Gleitman, the butcher, they were looking for. While Helen lay dead still and hardly breathing, they pulled Benjamin out of his front door, and pushed and prodded him down the street to the slaughterhouse. There, one of his Polish co-workers was waiting to accuse him of ritually slaughtering animals in the Jewish way. The man looked pale, almost ill. Benjamin said nothing.

"So, you disobeyed the Fuhrer and continued this dirty Jewish ritual!" The soldier spat the words out. "You think it is so important to kill in this way?"

Something in the way the soldier spoke, and the way the Pole turned his head away, made Benjamin suddenly terrified. The soldier pulled open the door to the slaughter room and pushed Benjamin inside. There, lying on the cold slaughterhouse floor in a pool of blood, was the headless body of Shmuel. "He was slaughtered the Jewish way, with one stroke of this cleaver. See, his head was cut from his body in one swift movement." The soldier, only a boy himself, sneered as Benjamin threw up over the body of his friend.

"Come," said another soldier, "we will see what work the Fuhrer has for a strong butcher like you."

With jokes about how Shmuel himself had now become the kosher meat he loved so much, they dragged Benjamin off.

Helen, Leah, and Miriam waited all day for Benjamin to return. That night Helen picked up her father's guitar and played all his favorite songs, one after the other. All through the night, she sang, until her mournful voice became so hoarse it cracked into silence, and she fell into a fitful sleep. When she awoke, she was at first confused to find her herself clinging to her father's guitar. However, this merciful oblivion did not last long, and when she recalled what had happened she screamed his name. This brought Leah and Miriam to her side. For the first time Helen thought her grandmother looked old. "He's gone," said Leah. "They took him." Helen said nothing, but in one movement she broke the guitar across her knees, and resolved she would never play again.

Shortly after this, Miriam fell ill. Helen visited her every day and, remembering how Miriam had kept her spirits up when she had typhus, she talked about what they would do when Miriam was well, the war was over, and Papa came home.

Miriam did not regain her strength, and she was soon unable to lift her head, even to sip the hot black tea that Helen made for her. From this point on, Helen did not leave her grandmother's side. Towards the end she climbed into the bed with *Bubbe* Miriam and lay there holding her.

When Miriam sensed her last few hours had come, she gently bade her granddaughter good-bye. "I would love to see the end of Hitler," she said, "but I won't. But you, *Maminu*, you will. I am dying, and you will go on living. You will live a long life and be happy."

She took out the silver earrings she always wore and asked Helen to put them on. Then sounding like herself for the first time in weeks she said, "Before I die I need you to make me a promise. Promise me now, that you will always light the *Shabbat* candles, and then I promise you that you will have beautiful children, and good children." Helen nodded wordlessly. "Every *Shabbos*, in your home, you must light the candles. Promise me."

"I will, Bubbe, I will. I promise."

Bubbe embraced Helen, held her in her arms, and whispered to her throughout the night. "*Maminu*, I will always be with you. Terrible things will happen, but you must never despair. I will always be with you. *Hashem* will always be with you and you will live."

Just before dawn Helen heard her grandmother let the last breath of life out of her body. This was followed by a moment of stillness. In the silence a sense of power and peace flowed through Helen.

It filled her up.

She felt whole and complete.

At that moment she knew with utter certainty that she would never be entirely alone again, and that her Bubbe's soul had become her guardian angel, the spirit that would guide her and keep her safe for the rest of her life.

In return for a sizable portion of the money Benjamin had saved, Moses Merin arranged for Helen to work in the nearby town of Skopek where a furniture factory needed workers because the men had been deported the day before. The next day Helen discovered that her good friend, Gutcha Furlonger, was also going to work at the factory. Helen had no doubt this was Miriam's first act as her guardian angel.

The girls worked hard. They had to maintain the production quota of the men they replaced. This required effective and efficient handling of large pieces of heavy lumber. Helen was strong and quick and the men liked working with her. The manager noticed that she was intelligent and responsible, and he soon made her his personal housekeeper and nanny for his children. It was exhausting to work in the factory all morning and then in the house in the afternoon, but Helen managed to win the love of the manager's children and the grudging respect of his wife. As the weeks passed, she and Gutcha began to believe that they would be able to live at home and work at the factory, until the war was over. On the long bus ride home they planned their futures. They would continue to work hard and the manager would never let them be deported. They'd stay together at the lumberyard until the war ended. Then they would go home. Their fathers would come home and everything would return to normal. Of course, they whispered, all the boys would come home too. The story didn't have much point without them.

In the meantime, roundups and deportations continued daily. In groups of four, SS men banged on doors and tore families apart. The people left behind tried to imagine where their sons, daughters, fathers, and mothers were going. There were rumors of course, always rumors, but none of the chilling stories made any sense. Why would the Germans take the trouble to keep such complete and efficient records if they were murdering the men and women they corralled so carefully? If their goal was to kill Jews, they could do that in the towns and villages where they found them. No one would especially put people on a train and take them away just to kill them. The obvious and most logical explanation for the deportations was the one the Germans themselves provided. Because so many German men and women were involved in the war effort, replacement workers were needed to do their jobs. Conditions were crowded and difficult and the work was grueling. Not everyone could successfully adapt to the change in their circumstances, so there were some deaths, but those who worked hard and followed regulations would be adequately taken care of, and eventually return home.

This is what Helen and Gutcha told themselves and each other until one morning, two pairs of SS men marched into the Skopek lumberyard and called all work to a halt. They informed the director that the Reich needed the girls at once and commanded him to send them outside. The director complied instantly. Helen looked across at him. Wasn't he going to explain that she was special, that she took care of his children?

Stony-faced, the director lined up the sixteen girls as impersonally as if he had been asked to set out sixteen armchairs. A soldier checked their names off on his list and then curtly instructed them to follow him out to a waiting truck. Helen still expected the director to intervene, but he said nothing. The soldiers stationed themselves around the girls and herded them into the vehicle. One of the older girls started to protest, but a hard blow to the head kept her and all the others very quiet.

When Leah heard the girls from the Skopek factory had been taken, she packed a valise for Helen and hurried to the deportation center. There she saw Gutcha's mother and other parents pleading with the soldier at the gate. He took the packages and valises, but would not give them any information except that the girls would be out in the courtyard soon. The parents waited there for four hours becoming more and more frantic as all attempts to obtain information, or negotiate the release of their daughters were unsuccessful. When the girls came out and saw the helplessness and pain on the faces of their parents, the hope that had kept them calm was shattered. All at once they were faced with the terrible knowledge that their parents were as helpless as they were. There was no one to save them. Each one of them knew the horror of being utterly alone. Helen began to sob hysterically. At just fifteen, she was too young to be torn from her mother like this. She ran up to the fence, reached through the iron railing, and pleaded, "Mama, come with me. Please. We can work together."

Leah, once again, denied the reality of her circumstances. "I can't do that," she retorted. "You expect me to leave everything your father worked for all his life and just come with you? He's going to come back and find nothing? No. I must stay here and take care of everything until your father comes back."

"Please," Helen begged once more, still clutching her mother's hand. "Please, I don't want to leave you." Leah shook her head. Her place was in her house. She would take care of it and there she would wait for her husband and daughter to come home.

Gutcha took Helen's arm. "We have to go over there where all those people are," she said through her tears, "and then we are walking to the station."

"How do you know?" Helen asked.

"Meyer told me."

"Meyer? He just had his Bar mitzvah. He's not even fourteen."

"He is here. Joseph too."

"Mama Please!"

"Go. Go. Quickly before there's trouble." Leah shut herself off from her daughter. "We don't want trouble. Go."

Helen opened her fingers and let go of her mother. She and Gutcha clung to each other and along with everyone else who had been selected for that transport, they marched to the station.

The men and boys stood in one line and behind them the women and girls tried to comfort each other.

"Board the train! Board the train." The SS guards repeated the order and started pushing and shoving the crowd from behind.

But there was no train, only cattle cars. The people looked at each other confused. What were they supposed to do? In their minds people did not travel in cattle cars. "Board the train. Board the train." The guards used the butts of their rifles to push the back row towards the tracks. Those in the front who were slow to understand what was happening stumbled and tripped over each other until finally, dazed and injured, they landed on the grimy floor of the cattle cars. However, as more people climbed in, it became clear that there was no space for anyone to lie or even sit on the floor. People pulled themselves, or were pulled by others, to their feet.

When there was absolutely no room for one other person, young Meyer leaned out and said, “Excuse me, sir, this car is full.”

He was roughly pulled from the car and slapped hard across the face by the soldier standing closest to him. “I will decide when the truck is full,” the soldier said. “This truck must take another fifty of you vermin, at least.” He pushed Meyer back in, laughing and mimicking him. “Excuse me, sir, the car is full.” His scornful laughter hurt the boy more than the rough handling.

CHAPTER FOUR

ZYBERSTOFF WAS A LABOR CAMP on the Polish-Czechoslovakian border. It had been established to provide the forced labor needed to build a railroad through the town. The manager was a Nazi functionary who was adept at obeying orders. He diligently went about his business, trying to manage his camp efficiently. His job was to keep his workers alive and able-bodied for as long as possible, in order to obtain the maximum hours of work from each prisoner. However, he had also been instructed to husband his resources. Therefore, he provided the men with the minimum amount of food and rest, which in his opinion, were required to keep them functioning.

The first nine hundred men who were sent to Zyberstoff, to build roads and lay railroad tracks, were not used to physical labor or rough living. They were professionals who exercised their brains and not their bodies.

Minimal rations and hard labor were for them a lethal combination.

Back home in Holland, Belgium, and France, these men had been doctors, musicians, actors, and business executives. When they were forced to leave their homes, they were advised that they and their families were being relocated to a town where they would serve the Reich in a manner appropriate to their qualifications. They packed carefully since there was a limit to how much baggage they were allowed. The men naively selected their favorite dress shirts and their wives packed just one pair of high-heeled slippers. Then, just in case they needed to buy favors, they tucked a small bag of diamonds or gold coins safely into the lining of their valises,

The wives and children never made it to Zyberstoff. Considered unfit for work, they were transported directly to the Auschwitz death camp.

Helen arrived at Zyberstoff at about the same time as the nine hundred Dutch, Belgian, and French Jews. Since she and her fifteen co-workers were the only females in the camp, they were assigned to laundry and kitchen duty.

It was Helen's responsibility to dole out the watery soup, which occasionally included a potato or a few peas, in such a way that there was sufficient to provide a portion for every man at the end of their twelve-hour workday. If she gave in to the pleading eyes of the men in the front of the line, there would be none left for the men at the end. She learned quickly not to make eye contact with anyone and just focus on trying to put at least one vegetable scrap into each rough wooden bowl.

Nine months later, all but ninety of these men were dead.

The polite, intelligent, and well-groomed gentlemen turned into frightened, confused, ragged skeletons. Many of them became too terrified and ill to understand what was happening to them. Each day they asked about their wives and children and requested transfers to more appropriate work camps. They traded their valuables for stale bread, potato skins, and other food scraps, but this did not save them from starving to death. The ninety men who remained alive were crippled, unable to work and finally shipped off to share the same fate as their wives and children in the gas chambers of Auschwitz.

Helen also worked in the laundry and cleaned the barracks. The soldiers liked her and sometimes gave her crusts of bread or lumps of sugar. She would find these tidbits under a pillow, or hidden in the bedclothes. As grateful as she was to receive the food, it was not nearly as important to her as the acknowledgment from the soldiers that she was a person, a human being; someone who could arouse in them feelings of pity.

She shared what she found with the other girls who also took great comfort from the knowledge that the soldiers felt sympathy for them. Anything that indicated there was still some humanity in the world helped them hold onto their hopes that this horror was temporary, and they would one day return to their normal lives.

The manager soon noticed that the red-headed girl was an excellent worker. She seemed to take the demands and discomforts of life in the camp in her stride. The SS *wachabender* noticed her, too, and ordered that she be assigned to taking care of his home and baby.

Helen believed that *Bubbe* Miriam had made this happen. And she knew she had to share her good fortune so when she cleaned up after dinner, she collected all the leftovers and hid them under her skirts. When the takings were particularly good, the girls would lay everything out on a bed and turn the few table scraps into a banquet. Occasionally, they even managed to sneak some of the food over to the men. The *wachabender* started calling her by her name, “Gleitman,” instead of his usual mode of referring to Jews by racial epithets, and this gave her hope.

The *Lagerfuhrer* requested that the SS send him another delivery of Jewish laborers. This time he wanted Jews from the east, laborers who were used to working for a living; farmers and butchers and those who were accustomed to cutting down trees and building roads.

The German High Command complied with his request. The SS transmitted the message to units occupying the towns and villages of Poland: Look for young men to build the railway line at Zyberstoff. In the town of Bedzin, they found David Pinczewski. His arrival in Zyberstoff changed the course of Helen’s life.

Bedzin was home to about twenty-five thousand Jews, who comprised more than fifty percent of the population. The Jews of Bedzin were doctors, lawyers, and businessmen who dressed in shiny boots and the latest cut in breeches and tweed jackets. Their houses looked like the homes in any European city, several stories high and packed closely together. David’s father, Solomon Pinczewski, had been living in Bedzin since 1925, when he and his wife, Dina, and their children, David, Rivka, Max, Fela, and

Meyer, had moved there from the small village of Czaunzwelky. In Bedzin, Solomon established a successful business, manufacturing and selling feather pillows and comforters, just as he had done in Czaunzwelky. His children all attended Rapaport public school and Gida Hebrew School, but since high school education was not available to Polish Jews unless they were very rich, the children started working when they turned fourteen. Until 1937, when he was drafted into the Polish army, David worked as a sales agent for his cousin, who made housing gutters. Fela held a prestigious position at the bank. Rifka had left school early, because at thirteen she had a stroke that left her partially paralyzed. Max worked with Solomon, and Meyer was still at school.

Unlike the Jews of western Europe, the Jews in Bedzin had always expected to be, and were for the most part, treated with respect, and anyone who chose to ignore this expectation was likely to end up with a broken jaw or find himself thrown into the river.

In August of 1939, the German half-tracks rolled into Benzin. That Friday night, as the Jews in the temple stood in silence for the *Amidah* prayer, a cry rang out from a young boy at the back of the shul. Having lost interest in the prayer book, he had been staring at the stained glass windows and the white curtains swinging beneath them. All at once he saw a flame leap from the curtains. Overcoming his fear of disturbing his father in prayer, he grabbed his sleeve and screamed. The fire spread rapidly. Soon the whole synagogue was in flames. The Rabbi and some of his congregants tried to rescue the Torah scrolls from the flames, and were burned to death. Those who ran out of the doors were shot by German soldiers outside. Eight hundred people died, but Solomon Pinczewski and his family were among the hundred who escaped and found sanctuary in the Catholic church next door. The priest took them in and hid them, although he knew that, by law, any Pole who was caught helping Jews could be put to death.

By mid-September, the Jews of Benzin had been forbidden to walk on the sidewalk, or sit on undesignated seats in the trolley. David's father advised his family to avoid going out as much as possible. He was sure this would soon be over. The Germans, according to him, were full of hot air, always huffing and puffing and threatening to conquer Europe. While he conceded that life had become frighteningly uncertain since the German occupation of the city, and that economic restrictions were making things very difficult, he was sure that

Hitler would soon be defeated and normal life would resume. Furthermore, World War One had been very profitable and he expected this to be the same. They would all make a lot of money off this arrogant German debacle.

Even when Solomon's house was burned down, he refused to face the severity of the situation. The family moved in with their good friends the Nunbergs and life went on. The Nunbergs' oldest son, Nusan, was a policeman and seldom slept at home, so he gave the Pinczewski family his room.

All this while, David was stationed in the barracks of Krakow, where Jews were a barely tolerated minority. During the two years he was stationed there, David learned many invaluable survival skills, including how to retain his self-respect in a hostile anti-Semitic environment. On the first night of Passover, he was just leaving for services when a young sergeant stopped him.

"Where do you think you are going?" he asked.

David reached for the pass in his pocket and handed it to the sergeant. "I have permission to attend Passover services," he said, forcing himself to be calm.

The sergeant glanced disdainfully at the pass and said, “You can leave when you have finished cleaning the floor.”

“Sir, I have just cleaned it,” said David.

“It doesn’t look clean to me. Clean it again.” Dropping the pass on the floor, the sergeant turned on his heel and left the room. No sooner had he left than David walked out of the camp too. As a consequence of this defiance, David spent two weeks in prison for insubordination. There he met up with an old friend, Potok, a trombone player he knew from Bedzin. The musician, who had been in prison many times, knew how to work the system, and David’s two weeks of incarceration were less onerous than his regular army duty.

However, soon after this he was involved in a more serious incident. On Sunday evenings, Polish soldiers lined up for an early evening meal, after which they were granted a couple of hours of free time. One Sunday, David was standing somewhere in the middle of this long line of 300 soldiers, when he was suddenly shoved aside by a Ukrainian boy who was tired of waiting. David, whose temper had always gotten him into trouble, shoved him right back.

“Jew bastard,” yelled the boy. The words were barely out of his mouth before David knocked him down and deprived him of four of his teeth. Immediately a guard came up to David, removed his holster, and arrested him.

The next morning, he appeared in court where the examining officer, Captain Schreiber, who was a convert, addressed him in Yiddish. "What happened here?" he asked. "Why did you hit him? This is a big problem. You knocked out four teeth. Who's going to pay to fix him up? Big, big problem."

David answered him in Polish so that the presiding Judge could understand. "He called me a Jew bastard." He explained, "I was protecting my honor."

The judge, in passing sentence, acknowledged he would probably have reacted to the insult in the same way and commended David for his courage. However, as David had transgressed, the captain was obliged to sentence him to another two weeks in prison. This time prison was a miserable bread and water experience, and yet he never regretted his actions.

When war broke out, David was assigned to be a gunner for a tank crew. The privilege of driving was always reserved for Polish soldiers, and in this case, the driver was the sergeant with whom David had had his earlier conflicts. They managed to get along. After all, they now had a common enemy, and David kept his temper under control. One evening, having been separated from their group in a Russian forest, the crew of David's tank pulled up near a farmhouse and rushed in to see what culinary or carnal pleasures might be available to them there. David stayed in the woods with the tank, the chance for a little solitude being more precious to him at that time than food, drink, or women. He was leaning against the tank, smoking a cigarette and thinking about what might be happening at home, when he heard a bomb explode nearby. He dived under the tank for cover, and when he considered it safe to look up, he saw that the farmhouse had been flattened and everyone and everything had been blown to bits. All at once he realized what this meant. He was free! No one would ever know he had not been inside with the others. Officially, he was dead.

He crawled into the forest where he hid until it was dark. That night he walked to Limbeck, a nearby Russian town. He knocked on the window of a Jewish bakery, and the owner let him in. He told the man what had happened and asked if he could stay with him for a few days. The man welcomed him, gave him bread and tea, and said he could stay as long as he needed as long as he didn't mind sleeping in the oven.

"I stop baking at about eleven o'clock," he explained, "and the ovens stay warm for a long time after that. I don't have a bed for you, but I am sure you could make yourself cozy near the oven." David stayed and rested there for a week.

The baker told him what was happening to Jews, now that Poland was under German rule. He advised him to wait out the war in Russia. David thanked him but said he needed to go back to help his family. They talked and drank and joked about David's nights in the oven. Much later, when no one laughed about ovens, both men remembered this week.

Traveling only at night, in the civilian clothes the baker had given him, David started walking back to Bedzin. On the road, he met up with two other Jewish boys, whom he knew from home, and from there the three of them traveled together. One freezing night they found themselves on the banks of a partly frozen river. The three of them stripped down, and holding their clothes high above their heads, they swam across the river to Poland.

They took shelter in a barn on the opposite bank, but as they entered, they realized the barn had been commandeered by the Germans. Small groups of shivering, barefoot, and terrified people huddled together against the walls. In the center of the room their fur coats, boots, jewelry, and watches lay in neat piles.

Sizing up the situation, the boys pretended to be Polish soldiers returning home. Pinczewski was not a Jewish name and the others had already chosen suitable aliases. The Germans put them to work making firewood from the telephone poles that had been knocked down, and then sent them on their way.

When he finally made his way to Bedzin, David barely took the time to kiss his family before he took his father aside to tell him how things were, and to urge him to take the family and escape over the eastern border, into Russia. He tried to make his father see that this was not another example of Germany looking for *Lebensraum,* this was an insane, powerful megalomaniac determined to destroy all vestiges of Jewish life in Europe. The stories that were leaking out of Germany suggested that this time even the most outrageous ranting and raving was being translated into action. Solomon hugged his son and thanked God he was alive, but he ignored his advice. Young people always overreacted. Besides, the idea of running with just the clothes on his back was impossible for him to accept.

Frustrated, David decided to bide his time. His father would come around. In the meantime, he made contact with the local partisans, and whenever there were rumors of searches or round-ups he hid on the roof of the Nunbergs' house. From there he first witnessed the Nazi inhumanity that was to change his life forever. Young husbands and wives were brutally separated and assigned to different labor camps. There were random beatings of anyone who did not move fast enough. Most frightening of all was the unruffled coldness of the SS soldiers. Boys no older than him laughed cruelly at an old woman pleading to be allowed to go with her children, and at a silent wide-eyed boy clutching onto the legs of his father. Often at night he saw thin frightened children, smuggled in from the Warsaw ghetto, hiding in alleys. He also watched starving local boys and girls rummaging in trash cans for scraps they could eat or trade.

The night the SS came to Bedzin looking for able-bodied Eastern European Jews to build the railroad at Zyberstoff, David was hiding on the roof. There had been rumors of a round-up, so David had slept up there and stayed hidden all day. Just before sunset two Jewish policemen came to his house.

"Mrs. Dina Pinczewski, your son David must report for work duty today."

She looked at the two men, relieved to see that neither of them looked familiar. "What do you mean?" she asked. "My son was killed in the war."

"Not according to this list," said one of the policemen. "His name is on here. We know he is alive."

Hearing this exchange, David felt dread tighten his stomach as he realized that someone had given him away. He edged forward and saw the taller of the men grab his mother's arm and pull her out of the doorway into the street. "You must tell us where he is," he said angrily.

"I told you already. He was blown up in a tank, somewhere in Russia. My son is dead."

"Yes, you told us that, but it is not true," said the soldier, twisting Dina's arm behind her back. "Until you tell us the truth, you will be our prisoner." He twisted her arm a little tighter and when David saw his mother wince with pain, he jumped down from the roof and declared himself.

"Leave her alone," he said. "I am David Pinczewski."

The soldier loosened his hold on Dina and she immediately regained her composure. She stared at David blankly. "Who are you?" she said. "I have never seen you before in my life. It is very kind of you to try and help me. Thank you, but you are not my son."

David was so astounded at first he could not answer. Then, realizing what she was attempting, he took her in his arms. "Thank you, Mama," he said softly, "for your love and for your courage." She started to cry and he hugged her tightly. "Don't worry, I will be back soon. My brothers and sisters need you here."

He turned to the policemen and said, "I am her son, David. Let her go." The policeman nodded curtly and David bent down and kissed his mother good-bye.

David was taken directly to the selection center. That evening at about six o'clock, his friend Nusan Nunberg came on duty. When he saw David, he paled but said nothing to him until he had a chance to speak to him alone.

"What happened?" asked Nusan.

"I don't know. They had my name; they wanted to take my mother as a hostage. Listen, I know there is nothing you can do to keep me from going tomorrow, but let me go home tonight, and I'll be back before sunrise. I didn't even have time to pack a bag or anything. I'll get some things together, sleep one last night in my own bed, and make sure my mother is all right."

When Nusan looked nervous, he took him by the arm and looked directly into his eyes. "I know they will kill you if I run away, and my family owes their lives to your family, so you know I will not run."

"Yes, I know," said Nusan. "I think they are sending you to a good place. I heard there is no rationing there, and they even give the workers chocolate." David raised his eyebrows at his friend. "Well, that's what they told us," Nusan said, discomfited. "Anyway, go into that side room. It has a back door. No one will notice you leaving. Be back before sunrise."

David did not spend the night in his bed. He prepared himself as well as he could for the ordeal ahead. His mother gave him her jewelry and his father gave him all the golden coins he could spare. He would use these to trade. Telling his parents he needed some fresh air, he slipped over to the house of one of his friends in the Polish Resistance. She promised to find out where this transport was going and to stay in touch with David. As morning approached, he packed some clothes into a bag, and then for the fourth time that night he tried to persuade his father to run away and take his family to Russia.

As for running away himself, David never considered it. He knew it would mean certain death for his friend, and he had faith in his ability to survive a German labor camp. After all he'd survived the Polish army. Could anything be worse?

CHAPTER FIVE

WHEN THE NEW CONTINGENT of men arrived in Zyberstoff, David Pinczewski was immediately singled out as a leader. He was strong and well-built and he had a manner and assurance that made people turned to him for advice. The *wachabender* noticed him too. He was always on the lookout for leaders he could use.

He called David into his office, offered him a chair, and said, "You look like a sensible fellow, a cut above the rabble out there." David, who was still standing, took a step back from the *wachabender's* outstretched arm and stared coldly at him. The manager cleared his throat, as he realized that this man was not the type he was seeking. Altering his original intentions, he assigned David to keep order in the work and food lines and dismissed him.

The first day the new men lined up for food, Helen felt hopeful as she looked at them from her serving hatch. They looked as if they were accustomed to physical labor and simple living. Even the way they reacted to the wooden bowl and gray soup was different from the way the business men and doctors had responded.

As for David, he looked like the boys she knew from home except he was more handsome than anyone she had ever seen in her life before. Her hand shook as she served him his soup and she felt the color come up in her cheeks. She watched him whenever he was close by and she saw he was good at his job, making his presence felt without being aggressive. One day, when everyone had eaten and it was his turn, she offered him an extra piece of potato. He smiled at and politely turned it down. And from then on she was in love.

"Ha!" she teased him mischievously. "You have just come from your mother's house so you don't need this. Fine! Don't have it, but just wait, soon you'll be begging for it!" David chuckled, as did the others who heard her, and the exchange was passed down the line. The men were amused, but more importantly they were reassured. If this girl was still able to be feisty and joke around, perhaps this place was not so bad. David's reaction was stronger than amusement or reassurance. The girl was very young, but she was already a woman. He was drawn to her eyes, which burned with a life force that was not obscured by the playful twinkle in them. He too knew he had met his *bashert.* The woman he was destined to marry.

Each day David labored on the railway construction, often doing more than his share to cover for others who were smaller, weaker, or just too anxious to function. He kept up his spirits by thinking about Helen and planning the short verbal exchange he would have with her that evening.

Helen's response to the attention from this handsome, young man was universal and timeless. She was being courted by a charming young man and every time his eyes crinkled up into a smile she felt her stomach flip over and her heart race. He kept alive that capacity for love and joy that she had brought with her into that sterile, bleak desolation. This nightly interaction helped her to sleep and dream of better days. It gave her the power to withstand the shock of her changed circumstances. She knew she had met her soul mate.

Night after night for two or three minutes at a time, Helen and David dared to believe in their future. Surrounded as they were by desperation, despair, and skeletal figures who thought each day might be their last, Helen and David remained optimistic. As the weeks passed they risked stealing a few moments together in the kitchen, or late at night in a bathroom.

What was so crucial to Helen's survival was not only that this handsome charming young man came to Zyberstoff, but that with *Bubbe* Miriam's help, she was able to love him there. *Bubbe* Miriam's spirit was always beside her, reminding her that she was there watching over her. Helen had no doubt that her Bubbe, as close as she now was to God, had made sure that David was assigned to this camp and no other. As she had promised her *Bubbe* she would, Helen had retained her belief that God was with her, had a plan for her future, and gave her the capacity for joy and romance in this man's company. And so she was able to submit to every indignity with a deep and self-forgiving understanding that resistance was useless.

She made two friends Esther and Anja, and the three of them befriended an older woman, Corolla, who had a weak heart and could not complete her assigned duty of scrubbing the kitchen floor. The girls conspired to keep this a secret from the guards and took turns to help her.

Besides the hard work, the three girls also shared the details of Helen's rendezvous with David. And they sang together. Late at night when they found themselves alone washing pots in the kitchen, Helen would start humming softly. The other two would join in, building up depth and tone, until their voices rang out, filling the room with sound. Their singing expressed their sadness, but also their hope and deep gratitude that they were still alive. Their world had shrunk to the goings on within the camp. They didn't know who was winning this war, but they had to believe this would soon all be over.

Helen also sang about her growing love for David Pinczewski. The strength and determination she felt in him and his warmth toward her gave her a place to escape to in her mind, a place where no SS man could follow.

Or so she thought.

One night, the girls were so caught up in hope and joy of their songs, they closed their eyes and took a short break from the never ending fear and vigilance they knew they needed to stay alive. Helen was singing her heart out and Anja, standing next to her, was transfixed, the wet pots forgotten in her hands. Helen's voice had transported them to a rainbow-colored place far away from Zyberstoff, when suddenly she heard a discordant clang. Helen opened her eyes and saw Anja standing to attention with her back to her. The pot Anja had been holding lay on the floor. Choking on her outgoing breath, she swung around and saw two Gestapo men leaning against the wall. Neither of the girls had heard them come in.

Helen held on to the sink for only a second, then forced herself to stand to attention. She recognized the tall officer they referred to as "the ox," and she begged *Bubbe* Miriam to help her stay upright.

The ox took a step towards them. "Stand at ease," he said, "and continue singing."

Helen took a breath and tried to obey, but her voice had literally died in her throat.

"Sing, Helen." Anja's voice shook.

Helen tried again. And again. With no success. Anja came to rescue, but her voice did not have the riveting resonance of Helen's voice and the ox told her to shut up and left. The beauty of Helen's voice like the chords of her father's guitar was lost to the world forever. She was never, ever able to sing again.

CHAPTER SIX

DAVID WAS PUT IN CHARGE of keeping everyone in line as they worked on the railroad. In time, he discovered that there were many advantages to his position. The guards did not question his walking around and they soon grew accustomed to him coming and going. Being outside of the confines of the camp enabled him to make contact with civilians and resistance workers. The project was being managed by a civilian foreman who was half German and half Polish and had no particular loyalty to either side. He was willing to help anyone who could pay for it, and he and David soon had a good understanding. Through David, the men were able to get letters sent home and have food packages, clothes, and most crucial to survival, shoes, smuggled in.

David made sure Helen and her friends always received enough food to keep them healthy and strong enough to work. Helen and David also took care of those who became sick, and the ones who had lost their minds and their will to survive. Because their lives were filled with purpose, daily life never became meaningless for them. If not for Helen, Anja, and Esther, who would help Corolla scrub the floors? If not for David, who would bring the food and messages into camp that kept so many alive and hoping? Having a purpose, a role to play each day was the most important factor in maintaining strength, hope, and the will to survive. With the passage of time, the worsening of conditions began to take a toll on the men. Many of them became sick and were too weak to work. Helen watched as the faces became thin and drawn, and the eyes took on the lifelessness of the eyes of stuffed animals.

One day, a young Czechoslovakian factory worker dropped her lunch packet as she walked by on her way to work. As she did it, she made eye contact with David for an instant. When the workers had passed by, he picked up the bag and found inside a freshly made cheese sandwich. He devoured it hungrily, relishing the freshly baked bread and rich, spicy cheese. The next day, the same thing happened, and the next and the next. She never looked at him again, or broke her stride, just let the bag fall from her hands as she went by. He teased Helen about this, saying he would never need her extra potato, because he had a "blond angel" taking care of him.

This continued for many weeks and the "angel" became the talk of the camp. However one snowy morning this brave young woman's luck ran out. Not wanting the food to be ruined in the dirty slush beneath her feet, the girl threw the packet a little distance away from where they were walking. This movement caught the guard's eye and he pulled her out of the line. "What are you doing?" he asked, picking up the bag. "What do you have in here?"

"It's just my lunch," she answered. "My hands were so cold, and I dropped it."

"No. I don't think you did. I think you threw it to these men. Why? Do you like Jewish men? Does your father know you like Jewish men? What about German men like me? If you give the stinking Jews your lunch, what would you give me?"

David, hearing this exchange, took a step toward them. Immediately the foreman laid a hand on his arm. "You cannot help," he said softly. "If you speak up you will be shot." David reluctantly stepped away instead of toward the girl and kept on walking until he was out of earshot. The girl was never seen by any of them again.

David knew that the foreman had saved his life and there was nothing he could do for the girl, but in his heart he felt dishonored. He knew that he had made a choice that would live with him forever. Furthermore, and what was worse, he feared that if he was to stay alive there would be many more such dishonorable choices ahead of him. His days of being able to do what was right were over. The realization depressed him and if not for Helen, he might have thought a life of constant moral compromise would not be worth living.

Sadly, Helen too began to succumb to the physical and emotional deprivation of Zyberstoff. She stopped menstruating and her stomach became distended and painful. She missed her *Bubbe* and her father and desperately needed some contact with her home, some proof she hadn't always been a prisoner. She knew David could send letters out of the camp, but the day after she asked him to do that for her, the whole camp had been forced to watch the hanging of a young man who had tried to bribe a soldier to take a message to his pregnant wife. The soldier, hoping to be commended for his loyalty, reported the incident to the lagerfuhrer. What the soldier didn't know was that the lagerfuhrer was waiting for a chance to show the prisoners that Jewish money was no longer the answer to Jewish problems. This young man trying to buy communication with his wife, gave him the opportunity he was waiting for.

To David's relief, Helen withdrew her request, but when time passed and none of the letters David sent with the foreman were intercepted Helen asked him again to please let her send a letter to her mother. David was reluctant. It was one thing doing business with the men, for of course both he and the foreman required compensation for their services, but to allow Helen to take this risk was something different. However, finally he agreed. In her desire to spare her mother, Helen wrote a cheerful account of her life in Zyberstoff, saying nothing about the brutality of her captors, or the risk she had taken in sending the letter. Helen did not tell her mother that this communication had to be kept secret and in her ignorance Leah sent through the regular mail a parcel to her daughter in Zyberstoff. The parcel was delivered to the SS *Wachabender* at ten o'clock on a cold Thursday morning. By ten fifteen, Helen's head was bleeding copiously from the blow he had given her as she walked into his office. He beat her viciously about the head, screaming, "Who sent this letter out of the camp?" Pulling on the leash of a scrawny, growling German shepherd, he repeated, "Answer me. This is a reply to a letter you sent to your mother. She says so right here! Tell me, whom did you give the letter to? You better answer me or I will command this dog to tear you to pieces." Helen felt the room spin about her. She could feel the blood dripping down from her head wound and she was terrified of the huge salivating dog straining at the end of his fully extended leash. She knew that if she told him the truth, the next time she saw David he would be hanging from his neck in the center of the courtyard. The *Lagerfuhrer* hit her again. "You will not leave this room until you tell us what we want to know. It is utterly forbidden to send information out of this camp. What did you tell your mother about this place?"

Helen wept. "I told her nothing, I didn't want to worry her. I just wanted her to know that I was alive, that's all."

"Who got the letter out of here for you?"

"I cannot say," said Helen, "I cannot say."

They left her lying on the floor, promising to be back soon. She forced herself to think. She prayed and asked *Bubbe* Miriam for advice. She had to give them an answer. What could she say? Whom could she accuse? Who could have taken the letter and would be safe from their abuse? Suddenly she had the answer.

When the officers came back, she sat up contritely and said she wanted to confess. She admitted that she had given the letter to one of the ninety Western European Jews, who had been sent away. She mentioned the name of a Belgian musician. She was sure the man was beyond punishment. He had been taken to Auschwitz, and as little as they knew of what was going on outside of their camp, they knew no one ever came back from Auschwitz.

The SS officer did not believe her story at first. He sent her back to the barracks and told her to return at five o'clock the following morning. She was once again interrogated and beaten, but still she clung to her story. Finally, they dropped the matter. Shortly after this the *Wachabender* was transferred to the Russian front and was replaced by the first of two genuinely kind Nazi officials with whom Helen was fortunate to deal.

The new *Wachabender* was a different type of man, older, kinder, and totally uncomfortable in his role. They affectionately nicknamed him *Velvelah*, because he only wore his SS uniform when he had official visitors, and otherwise he kept a low profile walking round the camp in civilian clothes and keeping order by making sure no one knew when he might appear. He made unexpected visits to the soldiers under his command, as well as to the inmates of his camp. Each day he became more and more dismayed by what was becoming of his beloved Germany. He was a warrior who saw himself as a conqueror of inferior nations, not a prison guard lording over weak, unarmed, starving men.

On one of his turns around the camp, he walked into the washroom and saw a couple embracing. He was shocked. They were of course breaking half a dozen rules by being there together. However, that was not what brought him to a halt. It was the smile on the girl's face. How could she smile like that in this place? Her eyes were closed and she did not see him, and the man had his back to him. So, undetected he left the room. A few moments later, he noisily returned. They jumped apart when they heard him and stared at him terrified.

David recovered first and pushed Helen away from him. "So you squealed on me, you bitch. Do you think this will make me leave you alone?" He spat the words out and glared venomously at her. "I'll make you suffer for this." Velvelah held up his hand, motioning David to be quiet. Speaking very solemnly he told them to return to their barracks at once and report to him in the morning.

All that night Velvelah tried to understand what he had seen. The two of them were undernourished, unkempt, and exhausted, but they had been kissing as if they were Clark Gable and Vivien Leigh. And then the boy had tried to protect his girl by implying he had forced her into this. He was trying to take the blame himself. Who did he think he was, Errol Flynn? He grimaced wryly. Herr Goebbels theories about Jewish men and women did not stand up very well to what he had witnessed. When the couple appeared before him the next morning, the girl was trembling and afraid, but the man looked angry and defiant. "What is your name?" he asked Helen.

"Helen Gleitman."

"How old are you?"

"Sixteen."

"Gleitman, this war is not going to be over for a long time. You and your friend must be more careful if you want to be alive at the end of it. Now go. You are both dismissed."

The story was soon all over the camp. Even before this, the love affair between Helen and David had been public property. It was a source of hope to everyone who knew of it. It was a life affirming beginning of something new, in a place where everything else was tainted with death. Everyone wanted to be part of it. After the incident with Velvelah they worked together to create safe places for Helen and David to meet. They invented a code word, "Siks" that was whispered to alert the couple any time they were in danger of being caught.

Shortly after this the foreman handed David a note that had been handed to him by a boy in the woods. Excitedly, David read that the partisans had stolen some false Gentile papers and were offering them to Helen and him. That night he crept into the kitchen and told her of the plan. They could disappear into the woods, change their names, and hide out until it was all over.

Helen shook her head. "You go," she said. "I cannot do that." David implored and pleaded with her, but she was against it. By now she understood the ways of Zyberstoff and she was sure that in the camp she could stay alive until the end of the war. Escape was a very dangerous proposition. Even if they made it out of the camp, which was unlikely, the idea of hiding in the forest was too frightening for her. And what if they were caught and brought back, or shot and left to die? She also knew that the other girls would be punished if she left. She elected to stay with what she knew.

In spite of her fear of being without him, Helen encouraged David to go. By this time, they had had many whispered conversations at the fence and secret meetings in the kitchen. They had developed a deep and abiding commitment to each other. Helen had endured days of torture without betraying David, and now she did not want to jeopardize his chance for freedom.

David was torn. He knew he should take this chance. At least it meant he would stay alive and then after the war he would find Helen and they could be together. On the other hand, he did not want to leave her alone and unprotected. What if things got worse and she needed to escape? How would she do that without him? He delayed giving them an answer.

In the autumn of 1942, the foreman returned from the Polish province of Katovice with devastating news. There were no more Jews in that area. Bedzin and Sosnowiec had officially been declared Judenfrei. “They have all gone,” he said. “Even the old and the children.”

The old people and the children, David wondered, what work could they be doing? The thought of his parents in a place like Zyberstoff made him shudder.

And what of his grandparents and brothers and sisters? Fela and Max would be able to contend with difficulties, but Rifka was partially paralyzed, and Meir was still a boy. Perhaps, he rationalized, they were in a factory somewhere, counting or packing or sewing. His mother could sew. He could not work and could not sleep, as horrific scenarios of what might be happening to his family ran through his head.

The truth was far worse than anything he could have imagined. On May 9, 1942, 800 Jews were deported from Bedzin to Auschwitz. On May 10, 1942, 1500 Jews were deported from Sosnowiec to Auschwitz. On May 12, a further 1500 were deported from Sosnowiec to Auschwitz. The May 12 transport was different to all the others. It marked the coming of age of Auschwitz. On this day Auschwitz became exclusively a *Vernichtenslager*, an extermination camp. On this day, there was no selection at the railway station, no lining up of prisoners who were fit to work, no beating or shooting or shaving of heads. These 1500 Jews were the first group to be sent directly to the gas chambers.

Before these mass deportations of 1942, Moses Merin had proposed that the Centrala Judenrat, rather than the SS, oversee the *aktion.* Long discussions with his committee members culminated in putting the question before the Council of Rabbis. Let them resolve the moral and philosophical dilemma of Jewish involvement in the selection process. Invoking Maimonides explication of *Mishnah*, many rabbis strongly disagreed with *Judenrat* involvement. Rambam was writing a long time ago, in a different historical period, but the circumstances were similar: what to do when a group of Jews is confined and told to hand over individuals to save their own lives. Rambam's conclusion was that Jews should allow themselves to be killed rather than collaborate with their enemies. Merin, however, argued that if left up to the Germans, the SS would deport leading citizens instead of the old and infirm. His approach was simple and pragmatic. He would sacrifice 50,000 in order to save 50,000. After much deliberation, the decision of the Rabbinic Council was to choose the lesser evil of Judenrat involvement, in the hope that Merin would be able to save a portion of the Jewish community. In May 1942, Merin sent deportation notices. They were met with passive resistance. Only 11 of 2500 Jews selected for the initial transport voluntarily showed up. Merin dispatched the Jewish police to round them up and personally supervised the arrest and deportations. In defiant protest, Rabbi

Englard strode at the head of the tragic procession. Nearly 15,000 Jews were deported. None returned. Yet Merin continued to dwell on thoughts of saving a remnant and justified *Judenrat* involvement in the deportations: "I am like the captain on a sinking ship," Merin wrote in his diary. "Only by throwing overboard a part of the precious cargo will it be possible to save the rest."

In August 1942, Merin supervised the gathering of 50,000 Jews from Silesia for an inspection. After the selection took place, less than half remained. Unbelievably, Merin continued to justify Jewish non-resistance and urged cooperation with the SS. "I am in a cage confronted with a hungry lion. I stuff the flesh of my brothers and sisters down his throat to keep the lion in his cage so he won't devour every one of us at once."

In June 1943, Merin and the top officials of the Centrala were summoned to a meeting with the SS. Reports indicate they were sent to Auschwitz where all perished. With the last round up of Jews on August 1, 1943, the region of Silesia became officially *Judenfrei*.

As 1943 became 1944, all hope for a speedy end to the war faded. The days followed one another in an agonizing mind numbing sameness. The goals of each day were the same: Stay alive! Stay out of trouble! Don't lose faith and don't stop caring about yourself and each other! Each day, from the five o'clock roll call to the blessed sleep that finally overcame them in spite of the hunger pangs and lice, was simply a battle to avoid dying. Many times during this time David could have escaped, but once he knew that all his family had been taken, he would not leave Helen.

On the morning of March 1944, the inmates of Zyberstoff were divided into two groups. One group went to Auschwitz to be gassed to death, and one group went to Blechammer to be shaved, tattooed, and worked to death.

CHAPTER SEVEN

DAVID PINCZEWSKI AND HELEN GLEITMAN were both in the second group and were sent to Blechammer. Because they were young and healthy and still of use to the Germans, they were selected to live and sent to Blechammer. There, Helen's role was to service the guards in any way they chose to use her. And it was in that place at that time that Helen was forced to find the essential survivor in herself. Her ability to adapt, to draw people toward her, to believe in herself, and to hold onto her faith in God were all crucial elements in her survival. However, many people just like her did not survive. Those who did had something extra. They made survival paramount. Surviving became Helen's only goal. Every action, every thought and feeling were evaluated by this standard, and no other. Everything that helped her survive was good and everything that might hinder survival was bad.

It was in Blechammer that she was forced to confront the truth of the horrendous rumors she had heard about concentration camps. People were tattooed with numbers, branded like they were cattle. Heads were shaved. Women were forced to stand naked in the showers before the lascivious eyes of German soldiers. Helen and the girls from Zyberstoff found themselves standing in line to present their forearms to a German soldier who took his tattooing very seriously. As each person approached, he checked their number and then neatly pricked each digit into their flesh. The girls from Zyberstoff stood together and distracted themselves by turning away and imitating the habit he had of sticking out his tongue, like an earnest schoolchild learning to form his letters. Then it was their turn. As the needle bit into her skin, Helen bit down against the pain.

The girls moved away and the soldier continued his task, meticulously branding each arm that was presented to him. Helen searched the faces of the line of men alongside them. She had not seen David and now she searched the line again, hoping she had missed him. She needed to know he was there. She could not trust herself to keep on fighting without him. Panic seized her stomach, which was fortunately empty. The girls huddled together, trying not to stare at the numbers on their own and each other's arms. All at once two burly kapos approached them and commanded them to get back into line. There had been a change in plan and the girls were to be reclassified and given a new number. Irritated by this break in the orderly flow of his work, the soldier roughly dragged his needle back and forth to scratch out the first number, and a second number was inked into them.

As it happened, the first number had assigned them to be exterminated in Birkenau. However, at the eleventh hour, the Lagaferer of Blechammer asked the SS to assign the girls to him. Why waste them? He could find a way to use young nubile girls, and they would certainly clean the barracks and fold the laundry more effectively than the men. The SS man laughed lecherously and agreed.

That night, Helen was first subjected to the dehumanizing indignity of public nudity. She stood naked and exposed. They shaved off her hair and pushed her into the showers. She desperately tried to cover herself, moving her two hands over her body as she realized that wherever she placed them, there was always one breast or her buttocks or something exposed to the eyes of the watching soldiers. As a traditionally modest Jew, and a virgin, she had never seen anyone else's naked body, far less exposed herself to the cold scrutiny of strange, hostile eyes.

After a few moments, the immodesty of the situation became less chilling than the anonymity of the shaved heads and nakedness. One hundred and fifty females had been selected to work at Blechammer. One hundred and fifty unique women had stood in line clutching their belongings, alone or clinging to friends or daughters. Each one was an individual, handling the situation in her own way. Soon all the women looked the same. Blank faces. Naked, female shapes. No one was anyone. The separate and unique individuals were lost to the anonymous herd.

They were all just part of a herd. To fight against the feeling that she was losing her sense of herself, Helen grabbed the hands of two of her friends. "Say your name, and mine, and hers!" They just looked at her. "Say it!" she insisted. She moved to the next group, and the next. Her survival instincts were now controlling her behavior. She found within her some deep unconscious understanding of what was required for survival and she made sure she got it.

The Lageraltester of Blechammer, Karl Demerer, was a Viennese Jew. He had started off as a kapo and had risen through the ranks until the Gestapo gave him almost full control of the day-to-day running of Blechammer. That he rose to this position was remarkable, but even more remarkable was the fact that he did so by remaining a loyal protector and defender of his fellow Jews. To the Gestapo he appeared to be a powerful, selfish man who had found a way to take care of himself. To the inmates of Blechammer, he was one of those unique human beings who become heroic in an environment where heroism is almost impossible. The greater the evil around him, the greater was his compassion and determination to make things better. He created routines and systems in the camp that seemed to be structured to promote efficiency, but were really in place to make life easier for the inmates. He roughly confiscated anything of value that the inmates still had, but he did not keep anything for himself. Instead he used the jewelry to bribe his Gestapo friends to give him more and more autonomy and power in the camp. Eventually, he was almost unsupervised, except for checks on the progress of the railway and production in the mine. As long as his camp met its production requirements nobody cared how he did it.

However, when it came to kapos who abused their fellow Jews, Demerer had no compassion. On April 1, 1944, Blechammer was put under the authority of the Auschwitz camp administration and became the satellite camp, Auschwitz IV. It became official policy to encourage kapos to abuse their fellow Jews for the reward of an extra ration of bread or water, or shoes that fit his or her feet. When one of Demerer's kapos took advantage of this he punished them in subtle but effective ways. He sent them to work in the coal mines. This was the most backbreaking work in the camp. To make things worse, by the time the coal miners got back, all the food was often gone. They complained to the Gestapo under *Untersturmführer* Kurt Klip, but the Gestapo just handed the problem back to Demerer.

For all his efforts, Demerer was unable to keep inmates from dying from the unsanitary living conditions and inadequate food. Nor could he prevent the horrific daily humiliations and random lethal punishments inflicted by the Gestapo. Every morning began with a five o'clock *appel*, a roll call, where prisoners were required to stand in a specific formation, in groups of five. Everyone tried to be in a row that was in the middle, so they wouldn't be noticed and bludgeoned by the guards patrolling the perimeter of the formation.

Upon their arrival in Blechammer, Helen and David had been told to keep their shoes together so they could wear them after the delousing and disinfecting procedures. However, this turned out to be just another ruse to confuse and disorient them. They were not given their own shoes, but instead they had wooden shoes of indiscriminate sizes thrown at them. This made standing still in the snow very difficult, for the shoes did not fit, and did not protect them from the icy snow. One morning, it was announced that a number of new regulations were being introduced. This included the anti-sabotage law that stated that any form of stealing would be considered sabotage. Anyone who transgressed would be hanged in the central courtyard.

Shortly after that, a man in David's work party realized that he was about to lose his feet to frostbite because his clogs, which were several sizes too big, kept falling off. He looked around for something he could use to keep his shoes on his feet. On the railway line where he was working, he found a piece of discarded rusty wire on the tracks. He picked it up and with frozen bleeding hands twisted and turned it until he could use it to tie his shoes. On the way back to camp one of the guards saw him showing off his resourcefulness and reported him. He was accused of sabotaging the success of the Germany's war effort by stealing wire, which was a scarce commodity. He was taken away.

The next morning the whole camp was woken an hour earlier than usual and forced to line up for *appel*. For about three hours they just stood there with no explanation until David saw his co-worker being led to the center of the square. A rough gallows was constructed and the man was forced to stand on a tall box while the noose was put around his neck. Then the box was kicked away. The man was so thin and undernourished that his body weight was not sufficient to break his neck at once. They were forced to stand in their lines and watch as death slowly claimed this so called saboteur. At about midday it began to rain, but still they were not dismissed. As the power of the storm increased, David, who was close enough to see the dead man, clearly could not take his eyes off the torn feet swaying in the strong wind.

By five o'clock many of the prisoners regarded the executed man with envy. They were cold and hungry and in great pain and this man was finally free! He seemed to be more comfortable and better off than they were. At least he wasn't feeling cold and wet and ravenous. Finally, the girl standing next to Helen could not stand it anymore and, taking a deep breath, she moved toward the electrified wire fence that would end her misery. However, Helen had heard her agitated breathing and was anticipating this move. She grabbed her arm and whispered, "No, it's almost over. Stay where you are." However, the girl had made up her mind.

"Why? What for?" she spat out in a hopeless hiss. Kicking off her clogs, she wrenched herself free and ran straight into the fence where she was instantly electrocuted. Two men followed her example, and the Gestapo in frustration, dismissed the inmates who had been standing in the same freezing spot for thirteen hours.

These suicides were not unusual. For those who could no longer hold onto any reason for living, watching a comrade being released in this way was often the last straw. For Helen, on the contrary, it was a reminder to be even more careful. Although she had never heard of Nietzsche, Helen was living proof of his contention that, "He who has a *Why* to live, can bear with almost any *Why.*" Helen knew exactly why she was going to live. She wanted to keep the spirit of *Bubbe* Miriam alive, to light candles on *Shabbat* in her memory, and to enjoy the full and normal life that had been promised to her by her grandmother. She knew this war was a temporary nightmare, and that it would eventually end. She was determined that when it finally did end, she would be there to marry David and have children and be happy.

Throughout this time, Helen had almost no contact with David. Occasionally they spoke through the barbed wire that separated the men and women, and sometimes at *appel* they were able to make eye contact. Knowing that he was alive was enough to keep her going.

By the end of 1944, the camp was full of rumors. The Russians were close! They would soon be liberated! For some, these rumors were literally a matter of life and death. The hope that the end of the war was near could prevent someone from wasting away and becoming a *musselman*, or running for the fence, or doing something to provoke a death-blow from a guard. Others were afraid. They had heard the Russians were barbarians who would rape and cannibalize them. Helen and her girlfriends paid no attention to these fears about the Russians. She had been raped more times than she could count, and the Russians were welcome to any flesh they could find on her scrawny body. Demerer was everywhere, encouraging his charges to hold on. "Stay alive, they could be here tomorrow," he whispered whenever he could. "Stay alive."

The Russians were indeed close. The winter of 1944 was one of the harshest winters of the century. The German troops on the Eastern Front were unprepared for such low temperatures and were freezing to death. Like Napoleon's troops 130 earlier, Hitler's soldiers were being defeated by the Russian winter. The demoralized Germans found themselves unable to prevent the Russian troops from advancing steadily westward. As rumors of German retreat reached Blechammer, glimmers of hope could be seen in the eyes of the prisoners.

On January 21, 1945, the inmates assembled for roll-call in a severe blizzard. They shivered in their prison rags and wooden shoes, and believed nothing could shock or surprise them anymore. Standing in their short rows of five, they reminded themselves and each other to endure this hardship for one more day. Just one more day, for tomorrow the Russians might come and liberate them.

Some of the inmates noticed that the SS man standing next to their *Untersturmfuhrer* was a stranger, someone they had never seen before. Some also noticed that there seemed to be more guards around than usual. After the *Untersturmfuhrer* completed his usual morning routine, the new man announced that he had very important instructions to give them. They listened dully as the man spoke. As the meaning of his words struck home, the courtyard was filled with a shocked silence so intense that it seemed even the wind had ceased to blow.

The snow continued to quietly fall as the prisoners held their breath while the instruction was given. "Today we will all leave this place. You will march to another camp where you will continue to serve the Reich. We will leave now. Start walking."

No one moved. Walk? To another camp? What other camp? Were they to just march off into the blizzard? What of the threadbare blankets and stale crusts of bread they had hidden in the barracks? And what of the sick who were not present at that morning's roll call? Were they to be left behind? To what fate? Those who stood close to Demerer looked to him for guidance, but he was as shocked as they were. Not one of the 4,000 prisoners moved.

"All of you. Turn and face the main gates. They are open. Rouse! Go now!" shrieked the *Untersturmfuhrer*, momentarily unnerved by the unprecedented mass disobedience. He looked around at the rows of prisoners assembled before him. For an instant he was almost overwhelmed by the wave of confused despair that rolled over them. Then he took a deep breath and drew himself up. He was a German.

A Gestapo *Untersturmfuhrer.* These people were nothing. “Guards, make them move at once. Everyone who doesn’t start walking immediately will be shot. Go! Walk! Now!”

The guards started beating the prisoners, pushing them toward the gates. Beyond questioning, beyond feeling, they were propelled forward. One foot placed in front of the other as a mindless response to being pushed from behind. They marched out into the driving snow. Immediately people started falling. Some lay where they fell, and some dragged themselves back to the lager to join the few invalids who had been left behind. Helen hurried to the front, knowing she’d find David there. Briefly their hands touched, but they said nothing. For thirteen days they walked. David and Helen spent brief periods together, but most of the time they were helping others. Their strength drew the weak and the frightened to them, and this, in turn, made them stronger.

Mostly they spent the nights huddled together in fields at the roadside, but one night they stopped near a huge barn. The prospect of getting out of the cold and spending a night indoors created panic as there clearly was not enough space for everyone. David grabbed Helen and, holding her above his head, used his bulk and strength to get them through the door.

Then he quickly pulled her to one side so they wouldn't be trampled on by the desperate mass of freezing, exhausted people crazed by the possibility of some warmth and comfort. In their efforts to get in, people climbed on top of each other, crushing and suffocating those who were trapped below. Consideration for others was a luxury they couldn't afford. Near Helen a woman suffocated to death, and when it was clear she was no longer breathing, the people around her said a cursory Kaddish and moved into her space. Helen and David were soon pressed up against the wall. The noise was deafening. People outside were pleading desperately to be let in, and others screamed in pain and terror as they were being crushed and suffocated. Eventually the guards who had made themselves comfortable in the farmhouse couldn't stand the noise anymore. Two of them ran up to the barn, shooting in all directions and yelling at the Jews to be quiet. As one guard reached the stable entrance, he hit David in the face with the butt of his rifle and knocked out four of his teeth. David barely noticed. He just spat them out onto the straw, grateful to have avoided being shot.

The next day, those who were still alive continued to walk. Helen found herself alongside two young boys plodding along with their father. She smiled at the younger brother. He told her that they had managed to stay together with their father since their deportation three years earlier from a little village east of Warsaw. The trio worked hard to keep each other's spirits up, even as they watched their mother and sisters put on a train that was rumored to be going to Auschwitz. As the day dragged on, the two boys took turns encouraging their father to keep walking. Suddenly the man just stopped and lay down on the frozen road. The boys stopped too. But the guards were not allowing anyone to stop for anything. One guard barked at the boys to keep walking. The brothers knew they would not be allowed to drag or carry their father along with them. They could keep walking or lie down in the snow next to him. They knelt down next to him, unsure of what to do. "Rouse!" shouted the guard. "Keep going!" The father kissed each of them on the forehead and told them to leave him and go on. The boys took hold of each other's hands and kept walking.

One of the most common disasters that befell the marching prisoners was the loss of their shoes. When this happened to Umek, a young friend of Helen, he also lost his mind. He knew that in Zyberstoff, and to a lesser extent in Blechammer, Helen's boyfriend could get almost anything. So when he lost his shoes on the march he asked Helen to tell David to get him some new ones. She explained that David was as helpless as the rest of them; he had no contact with the partisans and nothing to use for bribes except for a few broken cigarettes. Umek could not believe this. As one by one his toes froze and fell off, he grew more and more angry and abusive toward Helen.

On February 2, about 3000 of the 4000 prisoners who had begun the march reached Gross Rosen concentration camp. Helen was delirious with thirst. She approached everyone she saw and pleaded for water. She offered the broken cigarettes as a trade and cried with gratitude when a woman took the cigarettes from her. She told Helen to wait for her in the toilet hut until she came back with the water. Helen waited and waited, but she never returned. This betrayal as much as her state of dehydration left Helen distraught.

She stumbled out of the toilet and crumpled down onto the freezing ground, sure that it was all over for her. Suddenly she felt a cold hand on her cheek. She opened her eyes to see *Bubbe* Miriam leaning over her and covering her face in snowflakes. She felt them on her lips and opened her mouth to catch them on her tongue. The sensation of water in her mouth revived her a little and she crawled over to a woman who was sitting close to her and began to lick the snow off her arms. A third woman approached and soon they had set up a system. The women all lay on the ground, close to one another, on their bellies. As the snow fell, they licked it off one another's backs. Both the liquid they craved, and the cooperative way in which they took it in, saved their lives. The sudden unexpected snowfall was manna from heaven, proof that God had not forsaken them. For Helen it was a reminder that Miriam was still with her, guiding her, showing her how the snow could save her life.

For five more days they squatted in Gross-Rosen. Then the men were put in cattle trucks bound for Buchenwald, and the women were taken to Bergen-Belsen.

In February of 1945, when they arrived in Bergen-Belsen, it was already overcrowded to the point where inmates lay five or six, to a bunk. In spite of this, prisoners who were evacuated from camps in the Eastern Europe, continued to be sent to Bergen-Belsen. These included 20,000 women from Auschwitz and Buchenwald as well as thousands of male prisoners from Sachsenhausen, and the men's section of Buchenwald. The camp administration did not lift a finger to house the prisoners who were streaming in. Most of them had no roof over their heads and no water or food. There was total chaos in the camp and the typhus epidemic was at its height. From January to mid-April of that year 35,000 people died in Bergen-Belsen.

Helen had typhus too. She lay on her bunk with the other sick women and when one of them died, the body was pushed off the bunk onto the floor. From there it was thrown outside onto the snow where it lay with the other bodies like sacks of garbage. Indeed, the corpses bore a far closer resemblance to sacks than to human bodies.

Hunger was the force driving the behavior of all prisoners who had not given up the fight. Each day Helen dragged herself to the kitchen and asked if she could clean the floor or wash pots in the hope that she might find scraps of food and some water. They were given one meal a day; a small portion of half-cooked sand-filled spinach and a piece of bread.

One day Helen and a friend did get into the kitchen, and what was more, they each managed to steal a stale potato and hide it in their clothing. They left the kitchen with the light of success and anticipation shining in their eyes. It was this look that was their downfall. A female kapo noticed the shine in the usually dead eyes of these women, and this aroused her suspicions. She approached them and

Helen's companion panicked and dropped the potato. The kapo who had lost all traces of humanity by this time was infuriated by the defiance this theft revealed. Her eyes narrowed. She grabbed the girl and beat her on the head with the truncheon she carried. When the girl fell down, she pushed her face into a puddle of dirty water on the ground. She stepped on her head, stepping and stepping, until the girl drowned. Helen stood by, unable to do anything, her two potatoes hidden in her pants. She knew these two potatoes were life for her and the girls with whom she would share them. Any move she made to help would mean death for her.

This was one of the occasions where nothing but her own survival could be allowed to govern Helen's choices, or she would have perished. Each decision was unique and separate unto itself. There was no formula, no accepted right and wrong. If someone grabbed her piece of bread she had to decide instantly. Should she fight to get it back and risk being killed for it, or give it up and risk getting that much closer to starvation? She also had to decide how to eat each piece of bread she was given. Should she swallow it all at once to stop the hunger pangs for a moment, or save it to eat one crumb at a time during the day? If she had a bigger piece of bread, should she share it for the moment of intimacy that increased her will to live, or eat it all for the nutrition? Those who took dry bread from the bunks and bodies of the dead and urinated on it to make it soft enough to eat made her wonder if she should do that too. Would this act save her, or would it take away the last vestiges of pride that kept her fighting for her life? At every moment, every decision had to be evaluated in terms not only of physical needs but the spiritual, psychological, and emotional factors that were required to maintain the will to live.

Talking about food became a way to stave off hunger. Sometimes talk of favorite foods and remembered meals gave temporary respite from the craving. When this failed, chewing on wooden shoes and imagining it was food often helped. Food and drink were everything. Some prisoners pulled out their hair and threw it into the plate of a neighbor. They hoped that the lice ridden hair would cause the neighbor to be unable to eat the soup. Then the instigator of this action would eat the soup himself.

Every day Helen dragged herself off to the kitchen in search of potato skins or other scraps. She wrapped herself in her coat that had once been blue but was now gray with lice. Every day she stood in line at the kitchen door with anyone who was still trying to stay alive. Every day she became weaker and had increasing difficulty in keeping her place. She was constantly being pushed backwards from the door. Finally, one day, unable to keep her balance, she fell. The same kapo who had murdered her friend yelled at her for messing up the line. Grabbing Helen's arm, she demanded that she repeat her number. Helen was so exhausted she became confused. After repeating the number countless times each day, her mind shut down and she could not remember it. This enraged the kapo, who thought she was being intentionally defiant. She slapped Helen across the face so hard that she knocked her over. Helen fell to the floor and cut open her head. Disgusted the kapo turned on her heel and stomped off. Helen lay bleeding into the snow. As soon as it was dark, her roommates came out and dragged her inside. They tried to clean the wound, but there was no water. The wound became infected and then the lice moved in. Soon she had a huge pus filled swelling on her head. She became feverish and could not leave her bunk. All day she lay there repeating, "I'm gonna make it. I am." Some shook their heads at her in sympathy, but others too exhausted and despairing to keep hoping found her hope unbearable. "Be quiet," they said. "You think you're going to survive and find your boyfriend and everything. Well, forget it. It's not going to happen. We are all going to die here."

"No, you're wrong," Helen croaked hoarsely. "I am gonna live and I will find David, and get married, and have children. I'm gonna put all this behind me one day and have a normal life. I am."

As the days passed Helen became weaker and slipped in and out of consciousness, so that on the night of April 24, 1945, she was only vaguely aware of the frenzied chaos that filled the camp. There were planes overhead and speculation all around her. "Could this be the British, or the Americans?"

The next morning, she was struck by a silence so complete and powerful that it permeated her consciousness. There was no one shouting orders, no calls to *appel*. Nothing. Helen dragged herself up and went outside. No one but the inmates were stirring. Where was everyone? Suddenly they heard shouting from outside the camp, and then all at once they saw soldiers running toward them. British soldiers shouting, "You're free! You're free."

As suddenly as it had begun the shouting stopped. When the young English boys saw the thousands of unburied bodies strewn all over the camp grounds they were shocked into silence. The silence became even more intense when they saw the living. Sixty thousand living skeletons.

At this time, most of the SS guards in Bergen-Belsen were women. The soldiers hauled them out of the barracks and lined them up in a straight row. Then they invited the inmates to take revenge on their tormentors. “Kick them! Hit them! Spit on them!”

Helen took a halting step toward her captors. At nineteen years old she weighed no more than sixty pounds and her body was too dehydrated to make any saliva at all. There certainly was no possibility of spitting, and as to kicking or hitting, she was too weak to lift her limbs. She shook her head. There was nothing she could do. She just stood there and looked at them. Suddenly the realization dawned on her that her tormentors were now as helpless as she was, and they could no longer hurt her. She fell on her knees before the boy and thanked him and God and *Bubbe* Miriam. Nothing that happened had made her question her faith in God, and now she turned toward Him, in gratitude and prayer. She prayed that she would remain alive long enough to leave that awful place. She prayed that David and her mother and father were still alive.

CHAPTER EIGHT

THE SURVIVORS OF BERGEN-BELSEN who had no homes to return to were housed in the barracks vacated by the camp guards. This was a tremendous improvement from the conditions Helen had been forced to endure. The barracks seemed to be positively luxurious. There were no more than four women to a room and they had soft beds, food, and running water.

In spite of British attempts to take care of the prisoners, the death rate continued to be high. The food they craved so badly was indigestible to them. The prisoners had gone so long without food that their stomachs couldn't tolerate the meals the British provided. Tragically, many who had been able to survive incarceration, couldn't withstand liberation and died before the British doctors discovered which foods they could digest.

The British set up a survivor information office. Each day a soldier would walk through the camp calling the names of people who were being sought by relatives or friends. Since no enquiries came in seeking their whereabouts, Helen and her roommates were determined to become a family. Having been forcibly separated from their nuclear families, and uncertain of the fate of their real parents and siblings, they declared themselves related to each other. They would be mothers and sisters to each other.

Helen had lost all her body fat and her eyes were sunken into her bruised face. She moved like an old lady and her voice sounded breathy and weak. For the girls in this newly formed "family," helping Helen became a shared responsibility. Helen Boronstein and Rose Weizman, whom they called "Klana Roja" or Little Rose, begged Helen to go see a doctor regarding her head wound, but she refused. Her hair had just started growing back and she knew if she went to the doctor with a head wound the first thing the doctor would do was shave her head again. And how would that be appealing to David? Even though she had no information about where David was, or whether he had survived, Helen believed she would see him again soon. She looked skeletal, drawn, and ugly. Did she also now need to be bald!

Helen Wachslag and her aunt, Frances Drexler, who had come from Auschwitz, lived in the next barracks. Frances was older than the others and became a mother to all of them. She and Helen were to remain close friends until Frances died in 1960.

They all took turns taking care of Helen, changing the dressings on her wound and trying to keep it clean. However, in spite of their best efforts the infection spread, and she became feverish delirious. At that point Rose, ignoring Helen's protests, walked over to the medical center and asked an English doctor to please come and examine her stubborn friend. Rose also told him that she was equally stubborn and would not leave until he accompanied her to their barracks. The doctor agreed to return with Rose and he did examine Helen. More than that, he had her on her way to the hospital before anyone knew what was happening. As soon as he saw what was beneath the makeshift bandage, he blew hard on the whistle around his neck, summoning an ambulance. Then, before anyone could prevent it, Helen was whisked off to one of the many barracks that had been converted into hospitals. As the ambulance pulled away, the girls suddenly realized they had no idea where she was being taken. Rose and Helen tried running behind the ambulance, but of course they were too weak to follow for long.

In the ersatz operating room the British had put together, the doctor anesthetized Helen, cleaned out the wound, and then transferred her to the barracks that served as the hospital wards. When she came around from the anesthetic she found herself alone in a room with a German male nurse. She screamed in terror and tried to climb off the bed.

"Shh," he said. "Don't worry. I'm not going to hurt you. You've had an operation, but you are going to be fine. Are you hungry?"

Realizing she was very hungry, and reassured by his tone and warm smile, Helen relaxed enough to acknowledge that she would like something to eat.

"What would you like?" asked the nurse, relieved that his patient was lying down again. "Tell me and I'll get it for you. Whatever you want to eat, I'll get it for you."

"Soup and a sandwich," said Helen, "with lots of bread."

The nurse laughed out loud. "A sandwich you shall have. You are going to make it, you know. I can tell. You are going to be all right. You are going to make it."

However, the wound was slow to heal. Helen's ability to fight infection had been severely depleted. She was very weak and the infection raged through her body. The English doctor who had brought her to the hospital took a personal interest in her, and he went to see her every week until he was recalled to England. There was something about this young woman that intrigued him. He sensed in her a strong desire to fight her illness and he was determined to do all he could to help her succeed. Before he left, he stopped by to say good-bye to Helen and wish her well. To his surprise she became hysterical. She was afraid that if he left, the German doctors would no longer take care of her. The Englishman attempted to reassure her, but she would not be soothed until he promised that he would come back to personally attend to her when it was time for the bandages to come off.

When none of Helen's roommates came to see her, she realized that they probably had no idea which hospital ward she was in. She struggled out of bed one morning, intending to find someone who could help her contact the girls. To her amazement, when she looked out of the window she saw she was actually facing the barracks in which they all lived. She banged on the window until Helen Boronstein heard her and came running across the yard, but at the sight of Helen, Helen Boronstein fainted. From then on the girls came to visit often and, nurtured by their love and encouragement, Helen began regaining her strength.

When the wound was healed and it was time for the bandages to come off, Helen was very nervous. A nurse carefully unrolled each layer of linen until finally Helen felt the cool air on her head. The nurse gave her a mirror in which to look at herself and said with a twinkle in her eye, "I'll be back soon. I have a surprise for you."

When the nurse finally returned, she entered the room grinning broadly. "Sorry I took so long," she said, "but I'm sure you'll think it was worth the wait." She stepped aside and Helen saw that standing behind her was the English doctor who had kept his promise and come back to attend to her. He told her that she had healed well and the prognosis for full recovery was excellent. He advised her to remain in the hospital for a few more weeks and then always keep her head very clean and avoid hair dye. Overwhelmed with gratitude and relief, Helen thanked the doctor over and over again, and when he left she thanked the nurses and finally *Bubbe* Miriam for inspiring and guiding them all from above. Why else would the doctor travel all the way from London to Bergen-Belsen to see one concentration camp survivor?

The effect of the doctor's compassionate behavior was more than medical. It was for Helen an affirmation of human goodness. It was confirmation that the bizarre horror she'd lived through was over, that the Nazis were an aberration in human behavior, and not the norm. Most powerfully, she did not have to change her understanding of humanity to accommodate the last five years.

People were basically good.

What she had to do was erase the last five years from her mind.

Of course, now Helen wanted to leave the hospital and rejoin her adopted family in the barracks. The doctors would not discharge her, so one night, the girls stole a cart from the kitchen and crept into the hospital ward. While everyone slept, they rolled Helen onto the cart and wheeled her back to their barracks. There Helen healed quickly. The girls had made the barracks homey and comfortable and established a community.

They had a stove and they cooked their own meals. They were given some household necessities by the British and stole whatever else they needed. Klana Rose stole sheets, blankets, and pillowcases from the hospital store-room for everyone in the barracks. She was the most accomplished thief and took pride in her talent. It was said of her that "Rose could steal your eyeballs and you wouldn't know they were missing."

Every Friday night they invited neighbors from the nearby barracks, including friends from Bedzin like Shaya Zaks and Vov Nunberg, to come and eat *Shabbat* dinner with them. Their friend Yidel Potok usually prepared the meal, because he was the best cook. In this way they attempted to recreate the feeling of *"Shabbos"* that they remembered from home. Now that survival was not the only thing at stake, social interaction once again became the prime focus of each day. Amazingly, there in the barracks at Bergen-Belsen, surrounded by barbed wire and with hearts still full of painful memories, life was beginning to return to normal.

CHAPTER NINE

WHILE HELEN WAS NAVIGATING life and death in Bergen-Belsen, the final destination for David and the other men in the cattle cars was another hell on earth called Buchenwald. Typhus, starvation, and dehydration led to desperate violence over the smallest crust of bread or potato skin. The situation was aggravated by the many Russian prisoners who had been working in Germany when the war broke out. These people had no love for the Jews at the best of times, and now crazed as they were with hunger, they made it impossible for Jewish inmates to keep even their most meager rations. In groups of three or four, they attacked any Jew who had food and then fought each other for the booty. Many of them also resorted to stealing the livers out of the dead bodies that lay piled up outside of the barracks. These they cooked surreptitiously over a small fire and then ate the bloody meat.

From the moment Helen was no longer with him, escape was David's only goal. In order to get out of Buchenwald, he volunteered to move to a satellite camp where they needed workers in an armaments factory. Moving presented at least the hope of escape.

David, Harry Rosenberg, and Avram Seidenberg had no intention of actually building arms for the Nazis. On a particularly rainy day, after they had been marching for many days, the three friends pretended to collapse into a ditch at the side of the road. After a cursory prod with his boot, the SS guard closest to them decided they were not worth a bullet and he left them for dead.

They lay dead still all day, not even daring to express a moment of jubilation at their success. Only when the last prisoner had trudged by, and neither the moon nor the stars provided any light, did they crawl out of the ditch and along the roadside—always moving—determined to cover as much distance as possible before dawn.

At first light they saw what seemed to be a wooden barn in the distance and staying low to the ground, they dragged themselves to it, found it deserted and, utterly exhausted, slept for two days.

By this time Berlin was being bombed and the whole area was in total chaos. The three Jewish boys kept moving. They met up with some French prisoners of war. David traded a couple of razor blades and a small cake of soap for the Frenchmen's clothes. With nothing to distinguish them from regular prisoners of war, they now felt safe to go in search of food and a place to sleep.

By a stroke of luck, they found both. A German farmer woman needed help with her fields and animals. They stayed there and worked for her, even going so far as to sign up for food stamps. David called himself Kakowsky during this time and his friends took Polish names too.

When the area was liberated in February of 1945, the boys immediately set off for home. On the way to Bedzin, they met up with a "Russian" general. After speaking with him for a short while, David suspected the "Russian" might be Jewish. But as he was afraid to reveal himself to this stranger, he said nothing directly and only gave hints in some subtle comments. The general too began to risk a few hints. David bided his time. However, when the general said, "I have travelled all the way from Moscow, and I have not seen one living Jew," his eyes filled with tears, and the two men embraced. Wanting to reassure the old man, David said, "I'm from Bedzin. My whole family lives there. I was just on my way back to see them. Come with me."

The general shook his head.

"Come, my family will welcome you."

The general seemed unable to speak.

David waited.

Finally the general said, "Everyone and everything Jewish in Poland has been destroyed."

David refused to believe him. "You are lying," he said. "All Russians are liars!"

"It's true! And even worse than that, Jews who go back to Poland are being beaten up and killed. Every day! After all this, they still hate us." He sighed. "Please, go to Austria. The Americans will help you. They will even give you chocolate."

David suddenly remembered Nusan telling him that they would be given chocolate in Zyberstoff. He stood up. "I am going to Bedzin," he said. "Is anyone coming?"

David's companions—Harry and Avram—also didn't put any credence to what the "Russian" had told them. What he'd said was too shocking to be believed. They agreed to travel on to Bedzin with David.

They had been traveling east for four days before any of them dared to acknowledge that the Russian general had been speaking the truth. Reluctantly, David agreed with Avram that they should cross the border into Austria and make inquiries there.

The American soldiers did give them chocolate, but they didn't eat it. By now they had learned to store and save anything that could be traded. David traded his chocolates for coffee and alcohol, which were in short supply. Then he sold the coffee and alcohol on the black market and so managed to have some cash in his pocket.

The Americans confirmed the seemingly impossible truth about the annihilation of the Polish Jews—the horrendous reality that he would not find anyone he was looking for by going back home. They offered to help him look for his family and for Helen in the concentration camp survivor records. David thanked them but continued obsessively to ask everyone he came across for news of them. One day on the train to Frankfurt am Main he saw Eisenberg, his old friend from Bedzin and Zyberstoff. They hugged each other, cried, shook hands, slapped each other on the back, and cried some more.

"What are you doing here?" asked David.

"The British in Bergen-Belsen gave me information about some people who might be my relatives. But I have something to tell you. Helen is alive, in Bergen-Belsen."

"Bergen-Belsen," said David with a shudder.

"Yes. She is with me in the D.P. camp there. She is ill, but she is alive."

David turned to his travelling companion, a young woman named Franka. "Did you hear that? Helen is alive. I can't believe it. Are you sure it is her? Are you going back there? Can you tell her you have seen me? Give her a note."

"Yes, of course. As soon as I find out if these are my relatives, I am going back."

"Franka, do you have some paper for me?"

She nodded and handed him a page without revealing that her name was on the back.

He scribbled a note to Helen, telling her where he was and asking her to come to him.

When Eisenberg returned to Bergen-Belsen and gave Helen the note, she responded like any young girl might have in any century and under any circumstances. She and her girlfriends examined and analyzed the note. How sincere did he sound? What was the significance of the strange woman's name? One of the girls advised her not to go.

"How can you trust a man who sends you a note with the name of another woman on it?" she said.

"Remember what happened to me. You'll go there and see he has a new girlfriend. One with flesh on her bones and hair on her head."

Helen wavered. She knew she looked awful and she didn't feel she had much going for her if there was someone else in the picture. On the other hand, if David had another girlfriend why would he have asked her to come? No, she was not going to give David up without a fight. Who was this Franka, whose name was on the note paper? She would go and take her chances. Franka or no Franka.

Her friend Klana encouraged her to go and insisted to accompany her. There was not much they could do about Helen's appearance. Her hair had hardly grown back at all, and she was painfully thin, but at least they could make her something to wear. Rose went scrounging again and found a blanket that she used to make a skirt and a blouse and most important of all a kerchief to cover Helen's head.

When everything was ready, Helen and Rose went to the station and without bothering about the formality of stopping first at the ticket window, boarded the train for Frankfurt am Main. As they sat down, each in their own seats, their eyes met in silent recognition of other train rides taken without the benefit of seats. Neither needed to come out and say it. The painful memory of the cattle cars was too powerful to talk about and too recent to ignore. When the conductor came around and asked for their tickets, Helen lashed into him. "Tickets!" she said. "We don't have tickets. Hitler has our tickets. Go ask Hitler for our tickets." Needless to say, the discomfited conductor moved on to the next car.

Helen was still very weak and fell asleep soon after the journey began. The preparations and leaving had made her very tired. Rose didn't mind too much because she met a young man, Abramic, who kept her company. Three other young men who knew David were sitting opposite them and they tried to engage Helen in conversation, but she kept dozing off. Once she did wake up but kept her eyes closed and heard them making fun of her. "*Oy a Brock. Oy churbin*. What is David going to do with her? She's a skeleton and a *musselman*."

All at once Helen saw herself through their eyes. She felt herself flush bright red and her stomach turned. What was she doing? This was crazy. She stood up. "Come," she said to Rose. "We must get off at the next station and go back. This is a mistake. No one will want me like this. They are right. I am ugly and tired and sick. An old lady of nineteen!"

Fortunately, Rose and Abramic would have none of it. "Nonsense," they said, "Don't pay attention to these stupid idiots."

Abramic assured her that, as tired and ill as she was, she was still beautiful.

Rose reminded her that David would not be expecting her to look the way she had when he met her in Zyberstoff, and he would love her because she was Helen, as all the girls did. Helen hugged her friend and cried. The boys apologized for their remarks and finally Helen allowed herself to be persuaded to complete her journey.

When they disembarked at Frankfurt am Main, David wasn't there to meet them. The two girls looked around nervously, then went to the waiting room where there were at least some benches to sit on.

They soon heard a man's voice calling, "Helen Gleitman. Helen Gleitman." Helen and Rose looked up and saw a young man in the uniform of a policeman. Reluctantly she approached the policeman. "I am Helen Gleitman," she said.

To her surprise and relief, the policeman smiled broadly. "Thank goodness I found you. Don't worry about the uniform. I'm Dovid. I'm a friend of David's. He couldn't make it here on time to meet your train, so he sent me. Besides, I've got a motorbike. Tell your friend to come and I'll take you both to David's place."

As they walked to the street where the motorcycle was parked, Dovid explained, "I needed a regular salary and had always wanted to ride a motorbike, so I volunteered to work on the police force. I guess they figured I looked strong enough for the job. Climb on, girls, it's quite safe." As he helped them onto the bike, he said with an admiring chuckle, "Some *hondler* that David of yours. He's got a deal. He made some money trading booze and chocolate and now he's invested it all in coffee. Well, let's go."

The girls held on to each other anxiously, but soon began to enjoy the speed and the wind in their faces. That is until the wind blew the scarf off Helen's head and revealed her spiky, scarred scalp. Now she was so humiliated she hid her head in Rose's back. She was sure Dovid was laughing at her, and that David would faint when he saw her.

However, her fears were unfounded. David cried, hugged her, and kissed her head. He welcomed Rose, gave the girls his bedroom, and made himself comfortable on an old couch in the kitchen. Rose's friend from the train, Abramic, became a regular visitor, and soon two romances were underway.

David was very generous to both girls. His trading business was going well and expanding. When he came back from a trip with gifts of soft silky lingerie, the girls couldn't believe their eyes.

A few weeks later, Helen and Rose went back to Bergen-Belsen. David, who was now considered Helen's betrothed, came to spend *Shabbat* with them. This was a big event for Helen's adopted barracks family. Everyone pitched in. The "Chuchu" made soup and lokshen kugel on the heating stove and Rose managed to scrounge a tablecloth from somewhere.

David couldn't believe he was actually sitting down to a *Shabbat* meal, his first in six years. They lit candles, said *kiddish*, ate, said the grace after meals. They all cried as they assured each other this was "*Shabbos*" just the way they had done it in Poland. Hugging each other, the girls all promised to always stay close.

They said Kaddish for everyone who would never have *Shabbat* with them again.

After dinner, "Chucha" took Helen and David aside and spoke to them of weighty matters. She emphasized how important it was to get on with living, and that they both needed to remain brave and strong and nurture their love for each other. Most important, she said, was to rebuild the Jewish people by having children. She and Harry had lost their two children in Auschwitz, but God willing they would have another child. She insisted that Helen and David should not waste time. They had survived, they had found each other, they should commit to a future together and get married as soon as possible.

Emboldened by her words, Helen and Rose returned to Frankfurt am Main with David. The girls shared a rented room and looked for work, while David continued building up his trading connections.

One day, David came running down the street to their apartment in the middle of the day. Helen saw him flying up the street and she rushed out to see what was happening.

"Good news," yelled David when he saw her. She felt herself break out into a sweat of relief and sat down to wait for him. For good news she decided she didn't need to give herself a heart attack.

A survivor from Bedzin had told David that he thought his younger brother, Max, was alive and living in the town of Hof. Helen and David had given up all hope of finding any family members alive, and now there was a chance that someone as close as a brother might have survived. Helen scribbled a note for Rose, threw a few things into a valise, and they immediately took a train to Hof.

Upon arriving in the town, they were told that there was a Max Pinczewski who lived nearby. A few more inquiries gave then directions to the apartment and soon they were standing outside the door.

Helen knocked. They had planned that she would go in first to prepare Max for this surprise, but the minute Max opened the door and David saw it was indeed his brother, he rushed in behind her. The brothers' reunion was filled with such intense emotion that they were unable to speak. Waves of relief, shock, and gratitude, as well the intense pain of all they had lost, washed over them as they held each other and sobbed. When he could speak, Max implored David to move to Hof, where he had a good job. He was sure he could find good contacts for David. He wanted his only surviving relative close by and he begged them to come. David was reluctant to give up what he had going in Frankfurt am Main, but in the face of his brother's pleas, he agreed to move.

Helen Gleitman and David Pinczewski were married in the Hof town hall on December 2nd, 1945. Among the guests were Helen's "family" from Bergen-Belsen, many of whom now lived in the town of Munchen, just three kilometers away. However, there were also more than two hundred other guests. Because Helen and David's wedding was the first

Jewish wedding in Hof since the war, many of the additional guests were Jews from the area who simply wished to be present at a *simcha.* Then there were also those who came especially to hear the renowned cantor, Moishe Krause. Other guests, who had never heard of the cantor, were drawn into the hall by the sound of his powerful ringing voice. Curiosity also drew in many passersby, including a number of American soldiers, many of whom had never been to a Jewish gathering before.

Helen and David made a magnificent couple, both dressed as they were in splendid outfits lent to them by the mayor of Hof. The mayor frequented a restaurant where David did business. On many occasions when David was there delivering coffee and *schmoozing* with the owner, the mayor would join their table. Helen and the mayor had also made friends when he made a goodwill visit to the Jewish Committee of Hof, and he had been enchanted by her wit and warmth. He was so impressed by Helen's determination and energy that when he heard that she and David planned to marry, he loaned Helen a dress that had been his daughter's, lent David one of his own suits, and attended the wedding himself.

Once they were married, Helen and David found a room in a boarding house next door to the post office.

The landlady had been a Nazi and still held Bund meetings in her house. She only agreed to rent the room to this Jewish couple because the mayor intervened on their behalf. At that time accommodation was so scarce that Helen and David were relieved to find a place, even in such an unpleasant environment. They knew the landlady went snooping around their rooms when they were out, but they had no valuables and no secrets, so they mistakenly believed this anti-Semitic landlady would do them no harm.

One day Helen received a visit from two young men who knew her from Blechammer. They said they were on their way to Munich, but as their train didn't leave until the following day, and they would be sleeping in the station, they wondered if they could leave their suitcases with her overnight. Helen agreed at once, happy to have the opportunity to help a fellow survivor. They stowed their suitcases under her bed and left, promising to be back to retrieve their belongings the following night.

The next afternoon Helen had an appointment with the dressmaker. The newly wed Mr. and Mrs. Pinczewski had been invited to a wedding and she was having a new blue dress made especially for this occasion. The dress turned out just the way she dreamed, but when she returned home, excited to show off her new outfit, she saw two detectives waiting for her at the door. They asked her to accompany them to the police station to answer some questions. In response to her confused look, the officer explained that it was about the cigarettes.

"What cigarettes?" asked Helen, now even more confused.

"We found them, in the suitcases under your bed," said the officer. "Actually, your landlady found them and called us. Stealing American cigarettes is a serious offense."

"Stolen American cigarettes!" exclaimed Helen suddenly understanding what had happened. "Why, those bastards. I'll kill them."

At the police station Helen explained about the two men who had left the suitcases in her apartment. She signed a statement and they let her go home, telling her not to leave town. When David came home, she told him what had happened. He blanched. The thought that either of them might be incarcerated again was too much for him. When he regained his composure he said, "Pack everything. We will leave tonight. We'll go to Munich. It's a big city. No one will find us there. We'll change our names and start again."

However, when David went to tell Max what had happened and to say good-bye, Max talked him out of leaving. “You’re just panicking,” he said. “She’s a woman, and she’s pregnant. Nothing will happen to her. If it was you, it might be different, but she’ll be all right.”

“What makes you think they will care about her being a woman and pregnant? You know these German bastards. They’re all Nazis. Don’t you remember how those *bastards* treated women and children? Did you ever see a German who cared about anyone?”

“Please, David, be calm.” Max, who always was the calmer of the two brothers, reassured David that he was overreacting. “Those days are behind us. Things are going well here. I don’t want to lose you again.”

Helen, always an optimist, also saw things Max’s way. She persuaded David that she would be safe if she did as the police said and stayed in the apartment. She hadn’t done anything wrong, and she should not to act as if she had committed a crime.

Max suggested that David should go on a business trip for a few days to avoid getting himself involved in the situation. Helen agreed and in the end, David reluctantly went.

That very night, the police came back to the apartment and arrested Helen. She was taken to the courthouse, locked in a cell, and told she would be prosecuted before an American judge the following day. She spent a terrifying night alone, trembling with fear and forcing herself not to relive her war-time experiences. In the morning she met with the lawyer who had been assigned to defend her. He advised her to pretend she could not speak or understand German, as this would make her sound more innocent and vulnerable. This turned out to be the worst advice he could have given her. The court translator was anti-Semitic, misrepresented her statements, and the judge found her guilty. However, he did feel her circumstances warranted some leniency, so he said, "Because you have already been through so much, I will sentence you to only one year in prison."

The words came crashing into Helen's brain. One year in prison! He was saying that she would be locked up again—for a year! Fall, winter, spring, and summer. If she didn't miscarry, her baby would be born in prison. "No!" she screamed, running toward him. "I have done nothing wrong and you cannot do this to me. If you do, you will be cursed until the day you die. You will never sleep peacefully in your bed again and will not have a moment's tranquility in your life."

The judge, who was collecting his papers and about to leave the room, was struck by the force of this tirade. He asked for a translation and when the translator gave him one, accurately for the first time that day, he looked at Helen and said, "You can appeal, you know. Talk to your attorney."

In the meantime, David had fled to Bayreuth, where he tried to keep a low profile and stay out of sight. He stayed in daily telephone contact with Max, who kept him apprised of Helen's situation. He frantically tried to make contact with someone who had connections with the American military government and could help Helen get out of jail.

One evening, while attending services in the Bayreuth synagogue, he met a Jewish army captain. David told Captain Coolly of Helen's perilous situation and asked for his help. Captain Coolly was, at first, not sure whether to believe this nervous young man, but after intensely cross-examining him, the Captain became convinced that David was telling the truth about Helen's innocence, and he promised to help.

The next morning, Captain Coolly called the judge, to whom he was superior, and ordered him to have Helen released.

Days passed and nothing happened. Helen remained in the courthouse jail, where she was well treated, but remained very anxious. She managed to strike up some sort of friendship with her cell mates who were mostly prostitutes and petty thieves, but she found she had very little in common with them. She told herself she could get through this difficult ordeal the same way she had gotten through Blechammer, Gross-Rosen, and Bergen-Belsen, one day at a time, holding onto the hope that each day would be her last without freedom.

The difference was that now it was not just Helen Gleitman who was being deprived of freedom, but her unborn child as well. She replayed all her conversations with Max to keep her calm. He told her help was on the way, that David's friend Captain Coolly had intervened, and soon she would be released

However, all her rationalizing fell apart when, one morning, she was informed that she and the other female prisoners were being transported to a women's prison. This was more than she could bear. She became hysterical. Being transported had terrifying connotations for her. She had been transported from her home to Zyberstoff, from there to Blechammer and Gross-Rosen and Bergen-Belsen She could not be part of another transport of human cargo. When Max came to see her that day, as he always did, she told him what was planned and he became frantic too. Where would they take Helen? What would they do to her there? She would surely lose the baby. Perhaps he shouldn't have talked David out of taking her to Munich.

By the time Max left the prison he was drenched in sweat. Helen could not be taken away. None of them would be able to tolerate the separation. He went directly from the jailhouse to the American judge's home. He banged on the door and demanded to be let in. The judge was entertaining a lady at the time and was not inclined to be disturbed. However, when he could no longer ignore the banging and shouting, he reluctantly weaved over and opened the door. Max wasted no time in stating what he needed. "Your honor, forgive me for disturbing you, but you must not allow this to happen. My sister-in-law is innocent. You know that. The American Captain told you so. And she is with child. She cannot be sent to prison. After all she's been through, don't do this to her."

Annoyed at having his evening's plans interrupted and having second thoughts about Helen's guilt, the judge furiously threw his glass of wine at the wall and grabbed the telephone. He called the jail house and instructed the guards that Helen Pinczewski was not to be transported.

Max thanked him effusively and rushed back to the jail house. However, once there, he realized that the judge's instructions had been ignored. Helen was being lined up with other inmates who were boarding the bus. Max ran back to the judge's house and not concerning himself with decorum, ran right into the bedroom screaming, "You must come. They're putting her on the bus."

This was the last straw for the judge. He pulled on his pants, grabbed his revolver, and jumped into his jeep. Barely able to stay on the road he sped over to the jail house and drove right into the courtyard. Shooting rounds into the walls and the ceiling, he yelled at the officials. "Are you all idiots! I said she was not to be transported. Release her right now."

In the face of this tirade from their commanding officer, the guards instantly obeyed. Helen was released at once, and shaking with relief, accompanied Max home.

A few months later, the true villains were apprehended. Helen's name was cleared and an apology was printed in the local press. Unfortunately, by then, the stress had caused Helen to miscarry. The judge apologized to Helen personally and said she shouldn't hesitate to tell him if there was anything he could do to make amends. Strangely enough this led to a long and fruitful association. The judge's secretary and Helen actually became good friends, and for an appropriate reward, the secretary managed to fix things for many of the Jewish people in town who came to Helen for help.

Helen refused to go back to paying rent to a landlady who had betrayed them, and so, once again they embarked on a search for accommodation. This was made more difficult because German soldiers were coming home and getting married, and so there was a dearth of living space. Helen, however, was determined. She went to the housing agency every day and finally, exasperated, they told her to try the house of Frau Hellenger.

Frau Hellenger was a widow who lived alone in a big house, but she had boarded up her windows and had no contact with her neighbors. She had refused all agency pleas to rent out space in her house. Helen asked for the address, sure she could persuade the lady to change her mind. At first Helen thought she had met her match. Frau Hellenger was as determined and strong-willed as Mrs. Pinczewski, and she would not even open the door wide enough to let her into the entrance hall. However, when Helen revealed that she and David had been liberated from Buchenwald and Bergen-Belsen, and that their present landlady had betrayed them, Frau Hellenger invited Helen and David in. Shamefacedly she admitted, "I didn't realize you were Jewish. Please come in and let me apologize on behalf of my people." Ushering them in, she added, "Please, sit down and let me explain." With tears in her eyes, she pointed at her dark rooms. "As you see, I have boarded up my windows and doors so that I cannot see anyone. I especially hate to see them parading around and showing off the furs and diamonds that do not belong to them. They are so proud of themselves while they live in the big airy upstairs apartments that were owned by the Jews whose clothes and valuables they wear so shamelessly."

Helen remembered that when she was a child, the Polish kids in Sosnowiec had taunted her saying that one day all the Poles would get the upstairs apartments and all the Jews would live downstairs. This brought back such poignant painful memories that Helen began to sob. Frau Hellenger apologized for upsetting her and scurried off to make some hot sweet tea. The three of them had a strange, stilted conversation, until Frau Hellenger realized that she would feel as if she were making some kind of amends if she opened her house to this young couple.

Helen and David moved in that very day and soon were followed by other Jewish couples. The house became filled with people and laughter. Frau Hellenger was overjoyed when Helen confessed she was pregnant. However, despite the comfort of her surroundings, Helen miscarried again.

June 25th, 1946, was a warm, sunny day. David had just led the local soccer team to another victory. After the game, a Jewish American soldier, Captain Katz, congratulated the team and said he'd like to take a photograph. He planned to send it back to The Forward, the daily Yiddish newspaper that was published in New York at the time. The team lined up and then, spying Helen standing on the sidelines, Capt. Katz asked who she was. She's my wife," David said proudly.

"What a photo opportunity," exclaimed Captain Katz. "David, ask your wife to come over and join the boys in the picture. We'll show the folks at home we have Jewish soccer players in Germany being cheered on by their wives just like our baseball players at home." Joyfully, Helen joined David and the rest of the team for the picture. The captain took down everyone's name. When he came to Helen, the captain said, "We'll put in your maiden name too, in case you have *mishpacha* in New York." Helen and David thanked him warmly.

With her ebullient personality, Helen made friends easily. Among them was a will to get a new start in life. Mr. Fuchs decided to loan David enough money to start his own business. Just as his father and grandfather had done in Bedzin, David began making pillows and quilts from goose feathers. They knew that if they stayed in Germany, they could live very comfortably, but neither of them wanted to do that. Even after Frau Hellenger suggested that David and Helen take over ownership of the house, Helen held onto her dream. She had to find a way to go to America.

CHAPTER TEN

THE YEARS OF MALNUTRITION and neglect had left their mark. Helen had five miscarriages. The doctors told her that she would never be able to have children. But Helen never forgot the promise that Bubbe Miriam had made before dying and knew that she would have children. So despite her despair and disappointment she and David continued to try.

At the beginning of 1948, Helen became pregnant for the sixth time. As the months went by and the pregnancy progressed without complication, Helen knew that she would soon be a mother.

On November 28, 1948, a Jewish male child was born in a Catholic hospital in Hof, Germany. Nothing about this birth was easy. The presiding obstetrician - Dr Meyer - was aware of the fact that Helen had endured years of deprivation and had lost five children previously through miscarriages. And he learned that David had survived the death march from Blechammer to Gross-Rosen. He knew that this couple had lost nearly all of their family and decided he would do whatever to could to ensure that this Jewish child would be born healthy. He stayed with Helen for more than 24 hours of agonizing labor, then finally performed an emergency C section. He found the boy crumpled up with the umbilical cord tightly wrapped around his neck. The doctor rescued the child from that predicament, but immediately faced another one. The child was unable to breathe and was turning blue. The doctor submerged him, alternatively, in hot and cold water, and eventually the boy took his first life affirming breath, thus continuing his parents' example of surviving against all odds.

On their eighth day of life, Jewish boys are ritually circumcised by a *mohel,* in aceremony known as a brit-milah. However, organizing a brit-milah in post-war Germany was complicated. There were no *mohels* left alive in the vicinity of Hof, so David had to travel to the town of Schwandorf to find a *mohel.* Helen was not well enough to go with David, so Max accompanied him. They met with the *mohel*, came to an agreement, and arranged for him to travel to Hof for the *brit.* The child was proudly displayed on a pillow by his uncle Max, who had the honor to hold the boy in place during the circumcision. The child was named Solomon, in memory of his paternal grandfather.

Helen soon regained her strength and put her energy into taking care of Solomon. David put his energy into building up his quilt and pillow business. Life took on the natural rhythms of work, family life, and friends. David continued to play on the local soccer team and Helen, with a baby in tow, was always there to cheer him on.

However, not a day passed when they were able to forget that they were living on blood-soaked soil. They couldn't help but look around themselves with a combination of curiosity and suspicion. Had the jovial men with whom David now played soccer previously been associated with the deaths of their friends and family during the war? Europe was full of ghosts and trauma. It was time to try and leave all that behind and begin a new life elsewhere.

While they were trying to decide how to facilitate a move to America, the decision was made for them. Helen's uncle, David Glatman (the Gleitman was distorted thanks to the vagaries of American immigration officials at Ellis Island) had come to America from Sosnowiec in the 1920s. He and *Bubbe* Miriam had hoped Benjamin would soon follow. However, Benjamin, reluctant to leave his wife and daughter, had hesitated for too long. By the time he made up his mind, Hitler had invaded Poland and the borders were closed.

David's youngest son, Seymour, enlisted in the US Army in March of 1943. He was sent overseas and saw combat in Europe. From the end of 1955 into the beginning of 1945, his unit participated in fighting the Germans last attempt to maintain military control of Europe. The Battle of the Bulge was to be the largest and bloodiest single battle fought by the United States in World War II. Seymour's division participated in an attempted pincer action against the surrounded German troops. He was part of a reconnaissance patrol that tried to pin down the enemy's exact location. Unfortunately their patrol unit was spotted by Germans troops who were reinforced with machine gunners. The Americans took heavy casualties. Only Seymour and one other soldier from the patrol unit survived. But they were unable to get back to their battalion and had to hide out behind enemy lines.

Because the patrol did not return, all soldiers were presumed dead and their personal effects were sent home with the dreaded telegrams. Back in New York, David Glatman was distraught. He had been hoping that while in Europe, Seymour would be able to find his relatives in Sosnowiec and send home news that some of his family was alive.

It was several days before Seymour was able to rejoin his unit, and several more days after that before David received word that the army had been mistaken; his son was alive. However, it wasn't long before Seymour's unit was once again engaged in combat. This time he was seriously wounded and hospitalized in France.

Seymour Glatman was honorably discharged from the army in April 1946 and was awarded a Purple Heart, a Bronze Star, and a Combat Infantry Badge. His orders were now to return to America, but he was determined that before he left Europe he would search for any surviving remnant of his father's family from Sosnowiec.

In order to get into British occupied Nuremberg, where the records he needed access to were stored, Seymour borrowed the uniform of a British soldier, and in this disguise searched through the records of the SS. His painstaking research revealed that Helen had survived the war and was in a Displaced Persons Camp in Bergen-Belsen. Unfortunately, by the time he arrived at the camp, Helen had left with David for Frankfurt am Main, and Seymour had no way of tracing her whereabouts.

Back in New York with his father, Seymour attended classes at City College. One day, his father rushed into his room waving *The Forward* and shouting, "Look it's my niece, Helen Gleitman! Look, Seymour, there's a picture."

The photograph Captain Katz had taken on the soccer field had caught the editor's eye. It was prominently displayed as was the article about David Pinczewski and the soccer playing Jews team. Seymour grabbed the paper. "Is this her? Benjamin's daughter, the one I looked for in Bergen-Belsen?"

"Yes! She's alive. It says she's married and living in Hof." Father and son had both kept hoping for news of Helen. A hope that became all the more fervent as they discovered that all their other relatives had perished, most of them in Auschwitz. They immediately took all the myriad of complicated steps necessary to communicate with Helen and to contact the various authorities whose permission would be needed to allow her and her family to come to America. They went to the New York offices of the Hebrew Immigrant Aid Society, known as HIAS, who asked how this refugee family would support themselves in America. This chance to help a family member was regarded as a *mitzvah*, a wonderful blessing. David immediately volunteered to sponsor them. He promised to take care of his niece and her family and ensure they would not be a burden to the state. Of course, he had to back his promises with proof that he was financially stable and with help from his oldest son, Paul, he was able to do this.

When HIAS informed Helen and David that they had a sponsor in America and should begin the immigration procedures, David and Max immediately set about ensuring they would not be separated. They contacted HIAS and explained that although Max had no sponsor, he needed to go to America with David. The Nazis had killed all the other members of his family and they had to keep what was left of the family together. A sympathetic HIAS social worker took care of the paperwork, and soon Max, his wife, Anna, and their daughter Dinah, who was a year older than Solomon, were also in the pipeline to relocate to America.

For Helen and David this was a nerve-wracking time. After filling out endless forms, they had to undergo extensive interviews with the US Army Counter Intelligence Corps, known as the CIC. They answered questions about their politics, their family in America, their goals and expectations. When they were asked about their values and morals Helen had a flutter of concern regarding whether she had been fully cleared of the stolen cigarette incident. But she controlled her face and her voice and didn't let the investigator know she was worried.

Next, the doctors took over. Helen, David, and Solomon were physically examined, X-rayed and questioned about their health. The doctors examining them made it clear that if they were ill they would not be allowed to emigrate. While Helen and David felt well enough, they worried that the deprivations of the war years and the extreme conditions in concentration camp might have left them with some previously undetected disqualifying illness of which they were unaware. After two agonizing hours, which to the nervous couple seemed like an eternity, Helen and David were advised that they had been accepted for immigration into the US. They both started crying hysterically. Helen felt like she had been granted an eleventh hour reprieve. Clutching Solomon to her breast, she mumbled prayers of gratitude that her son would grow up in a free country. She prayed to God, imploring Him to protect Solomon from all the pain and hardship she had endured these last six years.

They were told they would be notified, by mail, of their sailing date. Every day, Helen and David eagerly checked the mail, anxious that some unforeseen event might disrupt their leave. Finally, the word came.

They were cleared for immediate departure. Helen and David packed up all their belongings and said goodbye to Frau Hellenger and the Mayor and the Fuchs family, the judge, the soccer team, Captain Katz and all their other friends in Hof. The immigration papers advised them to go to Bremerhaven port, where they were to wait until there was place on a ship for them.

After hanging around Bremerhaven for weeks filled with fear that a last-minute hitch would derail them, Helen and David received permission to sail to America onboard the *General Omar Bundy*. The ship was to leave Bremerhaven for New York on August 20th,1946. However, when they prepared to board the ship, Helen and David were devastated to discover men and women were to be separated. They reassured each other that as it was only ten days and they could do it as Helen would know exactly where David was all the time, and she would be able to communicate with him if necessary.

The men slept in large barrack-like rooms, but David spent most of his time on deck, because he was too seasick to remain below.

The women slept three or four to a cabin, and Helen was fortunate to share with a friendly Polish woman who kept her company and helped take care of Sol.

With no other facilities available to her, Helen washed Solomon's diapers in their cabin sink and eventually the drain became blocked. The day after they reported the problem, two sailors were sent to repair it. They greeted the two Polish ladies politely in English and set to work. A couple of hours later they seemed to have made very little progress and Helen and her cabin-mate amused themselves by joking, in Polish, about the inefficiency of the ersatz plumbers. About thirty minutes later the job was done. Helen and her cabin-mate thanked the boys in broken English, but were mortified when in perfect Polish, the taller of the two said politely, "We will tell the captain that you do not think we should be sent to do plumber's work again."

The Polish lady was so embarrassed she covered her head with a blanket, but Helen apologized so sincerely and charmingly that the sailors were amused rather than offended by the incident.

Being on board the ship was the first encounter with the American way of life for many of the passengers. Not only was the food excellent, but the abundance, variety, and generous hospitality of the waiters and cooks convinced the refugees that

America was indeed “the Golden land.” Even though Helen was nursing Sol at the time, the kitchen prepared two bottles of milk for him each day, just in case she needed it. Each morning when the waiters brought the warmed milk to her, Helen thanked them and cried a little. As Sol sucked from her full breasts, she told him about the milk and how it was in America, and she thanked God and Miriam that their troubles were over, now that they were going to a land of plenty.

On the last day of the voyage, a severe storm tossed the ship about so violently that Helen’s Polish cabin-mate was thrown from her bed. Sitting on the floor in her nightgown she began to weep, seeing the storm as a sign that life in America was going to be as rough and stormy as the ocean on its shores. Helen helped her up. “Of course it will be rough, but we will manage, like we have managed before.” They sat together until the storm abated, and then they went up on deck and hugged each other as the fog cleared and the Statue of Liberty came into view. The sight of the statue had a remarkable effect on the passengers. Some laughed, some cried. Others stared silently, awestruck at the sight of the beautiful lady, concrete proof that they were indeed in America. Prayers of thanks echoed down the decks.

Seymour came to the pier to meet the ship and called out to Helen from the dock. He told her that he was able to recognize her by the child in her arms. "You carried the only butterball coming off the ship," he said gleefully. He took them back to the two-roomed apartment in the Bronx where his father was waiting. They talked through the night. Uncle David wanted to hear everything Helen could tell him about his mother, Miriam, and his brother Benjamin and everything that had happened to the family in Sosnowiec after he left. She readily talked about the death of *Bubbe Miriam,* and all the events surrounding the German invasion. She told David and Seymour a little about Zyberstoff and how she had met David there, and then described their wedding in Hof.

The intervening years were not talked about. The intervening years were not talked about. For those who hadn't live through what she and David had, there was no way to explain. She had no words to tell these people about the horrors of life in Hitler's concentration camps.

The Glatmans offered one of their two rooms to the Pinczewski family, and the two men shared the other one. However, Solomon was still not sleeping through the night, and after a few weeks it became clear this setup was not working. Uncle David was employed at Borden Dairy and had to leave at four in the morning to be at work on time. Eventually the sleep deprivation caused by Solomon's crying became too much for him. Seeing this, David began looking for alternative accommodation. Living space was almost impossible to find, but eventually David managed to negotiate the sublet of one room in an apartment nearby. The tenant charged them double the rent he was paying for the entire apartment, and David knew he was being cheated. However, much to his frustration, there was nothing he could do. Back home in Poland or even in Germany, he would have known how to avoid being caught in such a situation, but here he was an ignorant *greener* and he felt his powerlessness very sharply.

David found work in a sweatshop. His job was to pack feathers into large sacks and deliver them to a factory on the other side of town. Here they were dyed a variety of colors and used to adorn women's hats. His starting salary was twelve dollars a week plus an allowance for bus fare.

He could not survive on this salary so instead of taking the bus, he walked from 14th to 34th street carrying the heavy sack on his back and looked for other ways to save or earn money. When he was offered a job as a roofer he took it without knowing exactly what it meant. The work was grueling and relatively dangerous, but he could start at fifty dollars a week. Without telling Helen what his new job entailed, he took it, and soon they managed to put down the $800.00 deposit required to rent their own apartment. They moved to 12084 Hoe Avenue in the Bronx and Seymour and Uncle David were invited to share their first *Shabbat* in their new home.

One day, while Helen was pushing Sol's carriage down the street, she looked up and to her amazement saw her husband standing high up on the fire-escape of a building across the street. He was loaded down with a full bucket of hot tar and an assortment of brushes and other implements. As she watched, he climbed from the fire-escape onto the roof where he balanced himself precariously and began spreading the tar at the edge closest to Helen. At that minute, although he didn't know it, David Pinczewski's career as a roofer ended. Helen told him that night she would eat no food that was paid for by this crazy, dangerous roof climbing.

David returned to the feather factory, but a few months later he developed a chronic rash. A visit to the doctor revealed that he had developed an allergy to the feathers or to the dye, and either way he had to give up that job.

Their next venture seemed promising at first. Helen and David were given the opportunity of renting an egg stand at a thriving flea market. In addition to the rent, they had to put down a deposit for the space and purchase the eggs in advance. They were assured that the egg business was brisk in that neighborhood, and if it didn't work out the deposit would be returned to them.

By this time Solomon was four years old, and what he wanted most in the world was to please his parents. Without knowing any of the details of their lives, he sensed the deep sadness and debilitating anxiety with which they lived each day. He so wanted to make them happy; to take the worried look from his mother's eyes and take the angry twist from his father's mouth. He did his best. He stood with them at the egg stand and approached all passers by calling, "Fresh eggs from the farm. Buy from my daddy. Fresh eggs, come and see." However, he found to his dismay, that many people just walked by, seemingly disinterested in his eggs and his daddy. He kept trying, taking comfort from the proud way his mother looked at him and her praise for his efforts. His father was harder to impress, but he never stopped trying.

One day, as his father watched, he was so determined to make a young lady stop and buy, that he pulled both her and himself into the egg stand. The lady was very angry, but not nearly as angry as David. Devastated at the loss of a whole week's profit, David lashed out at his son, calling him a careless, inconsiderate fool. He would not listen to Sol's attempts to explain and laid hold of him so roughly that Helen had to stop pacifying the erstwhile customer and rescue her son. David's frustration came raging out of his eyes and mouth as he grabbed his son by the arm and berated his clumsiness. Helen removed Sol from his father's reach, and at the same time tried to soothe the shattered nerves of her husband.

This was a pattern that was to be repeated many times. In spite of his efforts, and to his bewilderment and pain, Solomon often found himself bearing the brunt of his father's wrath. However, he also knew that no matter what he did, his mother would always find in herself the energy to intercede on his behalf and to show her love and compassion for him.

It soon became clear that they had been conned into investing in the egg stand. The rent and the eggs cost almost as much as their income from sales, and they never managed to make a clear profit. They eventually gave up on the egg business, and the morning David went to reclaim his deposit he learned another lesson about life in the New World. It took all of Helen's calming powers to prevent him from beating up the con-man who blatantly denied ever having agreed to return the deposit.

Max and his wife, Anna, were also living in New York by this time. Ironically, having no sponsor had made things easier for them.They received full support from HIAS, who helped them both find work. One Sunday, Anna, who was working at a knitting mill, told Helen that she thought they might need additional workers at the mill. That was all Helen needed to hear. The next day, without telling anyone where she was going, she left Solomon with David for a few hours and found her way to the mill. She took the elevator to the manager's office and knocked on the door.

"Yes, what is it?" said a voice.

Helen took a deep breath and pushed the door open. "I heard you needed a worker," she said breathlessly. "I am a very good worker and I would like to work for you."

"How do you know you are a good worker?" asked the man, amused by the approach of this short, rotund earnestly smiling girl. For a moment Helen was tempted to tell him, but she had learned to be wary of telling people her history. For many it caused more discomfort than compassion. While she hesitated he added, “Do you have any experience?” She was prepared for this and confidently rattled off her answer. “Oh yes. I worked at the factory on 186th street in the Bronx, the one that burned down.”

He nodded his head. He had other employees who had worked there. “Do you know Anna Pinczewski?” he asked. “She worked there too.”

“Oh yes,” said Helen, “she is my sister-in-law. She told me about the job here.”

“Well, we might need a packer,” he said as he put his head out of the office and told a passing worker to call Anna. When she came in, Anna successfully covered her surprise at seeing Helen there and said nothing to contradict Helen’s story.

“Well, Helen, perhaps we might have something for you. I’ll call you on Wednesday,” said the manager. He didn’t usually do things in such a random manner, but something about this girl touched him, and he believed she would indeed be a good worker.

Now Helen had to find a nursery school for Solomon, for she had no doubt she would be hired. She asked the mothers in her neighborhood what was available, and that was how she got to hear of Mrs. Glick and her wonderful daycare facility on Weiss Avenue in the Bronx. The wealthy lady who had lived in this house had died some years before and decreed in her will that her home and her money should be used to provide a superior nursery school for children of working mothers. Helen visited the establishment and discovered that for just $8.00 a week, she could get excellent care for Solomon. She was particularly impressed that Mrs. Glick conducted a health check on every child each morning.

Sure enough, on Wednesday morning, the manager of the knitting mill called and said that although they no longer needed a packer, she could have a job as a floor person. She gratefully accepted the job and soon found herself standing all day packing shelves in the hundred-degree heat of the unventilated mill. She never complained and she did prove herself to be an excellent worker. The manger was pleased with himself for hiring her. He had trusted his instincts and it had worked out well. One day when she was rinsing her cup after lunch he asked her, "Helen, what does your husband do?"

"Oh, he's an engineer," she answered.

"An engineer. Excuse me for asking, but what are you doing working here for this wage if your husband is an engineer?"

Overhearing her, one of the other managers joined the conversation. "What kind of engineer is he? What does he do?"

"He measures the streets," said Helen. "Every day, he goes out, and walks up and down every street looking for work."

Both managers burst out laughing. Helen laughed too, and the men couldn't but admire the strength and courage that enabled her to joke about such a difficult situation. They knew she had a child. They knew how hard she worked at the factory and how little she earned. What on earth did she have to laugh about?

"Perhaps we could find something for him to do here," offered the manager.

David came in the next day and was offered a job as a steamer. This meant he had to steam press the garments they manufactured and deliver them to his supervisor ready for packing. He was paid for each piece, but any items that the supervisor felt were done too hurriedly were returned to him. He soon got the hang of it and was given the additional responsibility of training other workers.

David and Helen were now both employed, and Solomon was being well taken care of at the daycare center. For a short period, things seemed to be looking up. The problem began when David noticed that many of the workers he trained, who were new immigrants, known as greenhorns, were being cheated. The steamers delivered the steamed pieces to the supervisors who counted them and paid the workers accordingly. One day, a worker who had completed twelve items, came back and said the supervisor had counted only nine, and so only paid him for nine. David was infuriated. He told all the greenhorns to be sure to count their own pieces, and tell the supervisor how many there were. This annoyed the supervisors, who accused David of being a trouble-maker, which soon translated into an accusation that he was a communist organizer. Before he knew it, he was fired and forcibly removed from the factory.

David then decided that whatever it took, he had to acquire his own business and be his own boss. He was very proud and saw himself as a displaced upper-middle-class independent entrepreneur. He perceived all the ups and downs he had endured since the German army came trampling over his life as temporary setbacks in a basically privileged life. He refused to view himself as one of the down-trodden masses. Rather he saw himself as temporarily on the wrong side of the tracks. However, now he was forced to swallow his pride and ask everyone he knew for help. What type of business could he buy? From whom could he borrow money to pay for it?

CHAPTER ELEVEN

HARRY AND FRANCES DREXLER, who had remained friends with the Pinczewskis since the days of Bergen-Belsen's Displaced Persons camp owned a candy store in Queens. Although it had not been easy, they were making a living, so Harry introduced David to his broker. The plan was that David and Helen would buy a candy store in Queens and live in the back of the store until they could afford an apartment. The Drexlers would be nearby and give them the benefit of their experience.

The Pinczewskis had managed to save about $2000 from the sweatshops, and they thought they would be able to borrow another $2000 or $3000, but even the least desirable store in Queens required that they take over a mortgage of close to $6000 dollars. In addition, they would still have had to pay rent and buy their merchandise.

Reluctantly, they asked the broker to extend his search to other neighborhoods. That's how on one sunny afternoon they found themselves one sunny afternoon, driving out to a predominantly Italian neighborhood of Brooklyn. Accompanied by the Drexlers, they were looking at a store located off Fourteenth Avenue, on 86th street. They found it squeezed in between a children’s clothing sweatshop, a grocery store, and a gas station on one side. They found it squeezed in between a children's clothing sweatshop, a grocery store, and a gas station on one side, and an ornately appointed cocktail lounge, The Nineteenth Hole, on the other. Across Fourteenth Avenue there was a golf course and a park.

The broker nudged David. “Fancy neighbors you’ll have here. High class. The customers of the Nineteenth Hole, should I say, organized businessmen and their associates. They bring their women here too. High class.”

The store was fronted by an awning and a newspaper stand. The names looked unfamiliar. One of the papers was called, “Il Progresso,” not a name Helen had seen in the Bronx. Above the door, there was a Coca-Cola sign and a menu offering a variety of food and drinks she could not pronounce, much less prepare. The products Helen saw on the shelves, as she peered in through the door, had names that were totally unfamiliar to her. She shook her head, totally overwhelmed, and looked over to see who her neighbors would be.

In front of The Nineteenth Hole, she saw a woman of about her own age. The broker was right about high class. The woman wore shiny high-heeled shoes and a green velvet, hip-hugging dress. A mink stole was draped around her shoulders and the feather in her hat was dyed to match her clothes. Helen smiled at her, and the woman smiled back. A warm, almost sympathetic smile. Just then a tall dark-haired man burst out of the bar, grabbed the woman's arm, and propelled her briskly toward a waiting cab. When he turned his back on her to open the door, she lifted her middle finger at him, and looked over her shoulder to see if Helen was getting all this. She shrugged conspiratorially, and Helen grinned, gave her a thumbs-up, and chuckled softly.

At the sound of her own laughter, Helen stopped. She hadn't heard that sound for a long time. It reminded her of who she used to be. The Helen who was always laughing had been lost for a long time, but it was time to bring her back.

She walked into the store and instantly recoiled from the smell of moldy food and stale cigarette butts. No wonder this store was inexpensive. It was filthy. It was also very small, about fifteen feet across and fifty feet deep. David and the others were talking to the owners, Molly and Al Beck. Molly looked as dirty and unkempt as the store, and Al was a chain smoker, who thought nothing of dropping his cigarette butts wherever he happened to be standing. Al and Molly were offering to stay on and help. They knew their products and the neighborhood, and they volunteered to come to the store every day until Helen and David learned their way around. The agent beamed at David as if this was a wonderful bonus, but Helen wondered how much help such people would be.

She did not go over and join them. Instead she went to look at the back of the store, the part that would be their home.

It was even more squalid than the front. The small sink was blocked and smelled foul. The stench from the toilet was nauseating. The bathtub was covered in thick rust, and the showerhead was broken beyond repair. Helen swallowed hard.

She noticed that in the back wall, there was a door and besides it two barred windows that seemed to overlook a concrete patio. Helen wiped the dust off the windowpane and looked through. At first all she could see was a chain-link fence and the concrete outer wall of the neighboring house, but when she pushed open the door and stepped out, the sight that met her eyes lifted her spirits. Just to the left of the patio was a small but thriving vineyard and a vegetable garden. Lush grape vines climbed over the wooden trellises that had been set up behind the house and alongside the neighbor's garage. Between the grape vines, vibrant tomato plants pushed their way toward the sun. The fruit looked ripe and inviting.

The vines were being pruned by a grizzled old man, who raised his hat in greeting. She waved to him. Solomon, who had come up beside her, waved too. The man smiled and offered Solomon a shiny red tomato. Solomon hesitated, trying to decide whether it was safe to accept. Finally, with a child's unerring instinct for goodness, he walked over to the man and shyly took it.

Helen felt tears prick the corners of her eyes, as she nodded her thanks to the man who was obviously delighted that the boy had accepted his offer. The warmth and kindness of this man and the empathy of the woman in green made Helen feel hopeful. Perhaps they were omens of good fortune.

She closed her eyes and whispered, "*Bubbe* Miriam, this doesn't look very good right now, I know, but I think it's the best we can do. What do you think?" She stood quietly for a few moments, trying to feel *Bubbe* Miriam's presence. She heard Frances come up behind her, "Uhm, the Goldenna Medina," she muttered ironically.

Helen rolled her eyes at her. "Wait, you haven't seen the bathtub."

As Frances came up alongside her and looked out at the garden she said, "If you half close your eyes and squint at the vines, it looks a little like Europe out there," she said wistfully. "Harry thinks it's a good deal. Do you think you could stand to live here?"

"Chucha," said Helen, referring to her by the name she had used in Bergen-Belsen. Chucha sadly nodded her head, "You of all people know how much I can stand."

David and Helen moved in at the beginning of May 1954. Joe and Margie, one of the few couples who had befriended them in the Bronx, offered to transport them in their new Ford. Helen and David piled all their worldly goods into the car, and when the inside was full, they tied the few pieces of furniture they owned to the roof. Although David and Joe tied everything together in the most ingenious fashion, the roof was not flat, so the minute the car started moving things started falling. Every few blocks, David jumped out of the car and retied a knot, or repositioned a chair. The pandemonium was intensified by Joe's insistence that his new car radio be playing at full volume throughout the trip. The combination of Bill Haley and the Comets singing "Rock Around the Clock," Helen and David's excitement about their new venture, and the constant movement of the household goods created an almost manic mood in the overloaded vehicle.

Helen was optimistic about the move, and David looked forward to being independently employed again. The good spirits in the car were infectious and soon they were all laughing. David smiled down at his son. Sol, looking up at his father's warm eyes and loving smile, wished with all his heart that his father would always look at him like that.

When they arrived at their destination, Margie and Joe got their first look at the candy store, and they were shocked. They had not expected anything so small, dark, and depressing, but they quickly recovered their good spirits and immediately began getting the place into shape.

Helen had made some drapes and so the first thing Margie helped with was closing off the area in the back of the store in order to make it feel a little bit more homey. Their living space was about twenty feet wide and fourteen feet deep. They divided the space into a bathroom/kitchen area and two bedrooms. Then they began the daunting task of removing the grime, dirt, and dust that years of neglect had left behind.

Although they tried to find an alternative, Helen and David had to put their bed directly under a leaky skylight. As for Sol's bed, the legs had broken off when it fell off the car roof for the third time. David replaced the legs with some empty soda crates he found in the store basement.

When Helen put Sol to sleep that night, she remembered how comfortable her life had been when she was his age. She remembered that as a child, she had taken food to families who were as impoverished as she now was. "Well, it is true we have known better," she said to David with a sigh, "but let us not forget that we have also known worse."

She often put Sol to sleep with his favorite story about the time Helen hid in *Bubbe* Miriam's bed while the SS were looking for her. It was a story he had heard from the time he was old enough to listen. While other children shivered in anticipation about whether the wolf would eat Little Red Riding Hood or gobble up the three little pigs, he listened with bated breath to his mother telling how she, trying to look like an extra pillow, lay dead still under the covers while *Bubbe* Miriam showed just how brave and smart she really was.

"*Bubbe* is still with us," she always said at the end of the story. "Her spirit is always watching us and helping us. If ever you feel lonely or scared, you can ask her to help you." Then she'd stroke his head and whisper the words of the lullaby her grandmother had sung to her *Shein vey de livunaa Lechtug vi die erets.* She would have liked to have sung these reassuring words, but she had been left unable to sing by her experience in Blechammer.

Despite her previous misgivings, Helen was relieved when Al and Molly Beck showed up the next morning to help. Having only been in the country for a few years there was so much Helen still didn't know. And though she could speak a little bit of English, she couldn't read it. Which made for frustration and confusion when a customer asked for something and she couldn't find it on the shelf.

Most confusing of all was the array of mixed soda drinks she was expected to make. She had to learn that an egg crème contained no eggs and no cream. Molly Beck showed her that it was simply a combination of milk, chocolate syrup, and seltzer. Molly also taught her how to prepare limerickies, cherry smashes, malteds, and floats. It was with great relief that Helen discovered that "Denobilis" was not yet another drink, but a popular brand of cigars.

The pronunciation of English words that should have been familiar was another hurdle. The Brooklyn accents and wise-guy terminology of the area were utterly unfamiliar to them. David knew he often appeared as a bumbling half-wit to his customers, and this infuriated him. When he saw the disdain and amusement in their eyes, it took all his self-control not to grab them by the collar and teach them to look at him with respect. Instead, he had to stand by patiently, as they condescended to explain that "Between the Acts" was a type of cigar and not a heavy tool.

Unfortunately, Al and Molly had such slovenly habits and so little regard for Helen's housekeeping efforts that eventually Helen asked them to leave. She preferred to muddle through rather than have to be constantly cleaning up after the Becks. She dealt with the menu on the Coca-Cola sign by telling her customers, "You can have a cheese sandwich, or a cheese sandwich, and that is all."

Shortly after the departure of Al and Molly, Helen and David got to know the family of their next-door neighbor, Pop Fusaro, whose grape and tomato vines had so lifted Helen's spirits on that first day. Helen's unerring instincts had been right. The Fusaro family became the Pinczewskis' greatest source of emotional sustenance. The love and nurturing acceptance this family gave them helped Helen and David to begin to trust and interact naturally with the society around them.

Pop's middle son, Dominick, came into the store regularly to buy the Il Progresso Newspaper and Denobili cigars for his father. One afternoon, while he was there, a neighborhood thug came in and said, "Heh, you, make me a fuggen egg-creme and be quick about it!"

Helen, unaccustomed as she was to such profanity, became embarrassed and clumsy, which only increased the customer's impatience. His vocabulary became more abusive, and Helen spilled the whole drink. Dominick walked up to the counter and talking quietly and reassuringly to Helen, helped her remake the drink. After the customer left, Helen thanked him profusely and introduced him to her husband and son.

Dominick had already noticed that Solomon was expected to take a great deal of responsibility for a six-year-old boy. He was drawn to this wide-eyed child who didn't seem to have anything child-like about his life. When he came into the store, he often took the time to chat to Sol. Delighted by the attention, Sol told him all about his school, P.S. 229, and about Mrs. Gilhooly, his teacher. Sol proudly explained to Dominic that since his English was better than either of his parents, he helped his father check order and talk to vendors.

As Dominick spent more and more time in the store, he learned where this young Jewish couple came from, what they had gone through, and how they came to be running a candy-store in this Italian neighborhood. He was shocked. It was one thing to read about the atrocities of Hitler's regime, or to see newsreels of the liberation of the concentration camps, but to be standing with people who had lived through this and were still going on with life in such a normal fashion, created a paradigm shift in his understanding of the world.

He wrestled with the concept that people in his life, people he interacted with every day, had endured these horrors. He asked himself what he could do for people who had endured such pain when he himself had never known any real deprivation. As his understanding increased, so did his respect for their tenacity and courage. He was a devout Catholic who had never married and he wondered if perhaps God had meant him to take care of this family

Helen had no doubt that Dominick's involvement in their lives was a gift from Bubbe Miriam. One sweltering summer day, during the dog days of August, Dominick came in and said, "Helen, I'm off to Coney Island. How about I take Sol with me?"

She dropped what she was doing, went up to Dominick, and hugged him. "Oh thank you and God bless you. I don't know how I would manage if you hadn't been sent to help me."

At this time, Helen and David were working seven days a week from five in the morning until well after midnight when they fell exhausted into bed for a few hours' rest. They worked in shifts, so that the store was always open, and they never missed a sale. In addition, there were also the orders and deliveries and loans to worry about. They took no leisure time for themselves, and so of course there was no recreation for Sol. At school, he was able to be a boy, but once he got home he was a six-year-old working man.

Going out with Dominick, where the only goal was to have fun was an amazing treat for Solomon. For his part, Dominick found he had more fun when Sol was with him. He often dropped by the store, and if Sol could be spared, took him to the beach, or to a movie. Helen was greatly relieved to get him out of the heat and humidity of the store and was even more happy when, at the end of the day, he came home tired, ruddy-faced, and full of stories just like a "regular kid." She remembered how *Bubbe* Miriam had always made sure that she had fun as a child, and how she had insisted that her parents buy her ice-skates, or "sliding-shoes," as she had called them.

In winter, Dominick would rescue Sol from the monotonous, cold, wet damp of the store and take him out. They would sit on Santa's lap and gawk at the Christmas decorations at Macy's, or go to a movie or just make snowballs in the garden. He also enjoyed helping Solomon with his homework, a task for which neither of his parents had adequate English skills.

One Sunday, Dominick invited Sol to come and have lunch with his family. This was the beginning of many wonderful Sundays that Sol would spend in the Fusaro household. Pop Fusaro, who spoke mostly Italian, taught Sol to play cards. Soon he was a worthy Brisk opponent for the old man. Pop Fusaro also taught him to make home-made wine and he spent many happy hours watching Pop press the grapes. Occasionally, Pop would taste the fruits of their labors, and on those days Sol always won at Brisk. He also taught Sol to play Bocce in the park and Sol became quite skilled at rolling the balls just right.

Mrs. Fusaro, Pop's wife, had died tragically just a few years after her youngest child, Beatrice, was born. She had been a compassionate, generous woman. Now the children lived at home with their father and continued their mother's tradition of caretaking for each other and other people in need.

The Fusaros became Sol's surrogate family. Mary, Pop's oldest daughter, was mother to them all. She always had a pot of meatballs and tomato sauce on the stove for anyone who came in hungry. Frankie, the youngest son, was a veteran of the Korean War. Post-traumatic stress made him very nervous, but he was always kind and congenial. The oldest son, Pat, was a policeman. He lived on the middle level of the house with his wife, Olga, and their son, Joey. Beatrice was away at a convent. She was a novice and the family hoped very much that she would stay and become a nun. The Pinczewskis, especially Solomon, became protégés of this warm and generous family, who all spoiled the boy and tried to make up for the deprivations of his life.

Dominick was especially concerned about Sol's spiritual health. He worried that Sol spent too much time in the store, where he was subjected to the profanity and immoral behavior of the local hoodlums. Furthermore, on the streets and sidewalks of that rough and tumble neighborhood, there were questionable characters transacting, at best, shady deals.

While it was clear that David and Helen were honest God-fearing people, Sol did not seem to have any spiritual or religious understanding. Dominick longed to give Sol some of the comfort he himself derived from his faith. However, he was not sure how to approach the matter until they went, one cold and rainy afternoon, to see *The Song of Bernadette.*

This poignant film, starring Jennifer Jones as a Catholic peasant girl who had a vision of Mary, the Holy Mother, made a great impression on Sol. He was very moved by the story, and by the idea that there was a female supernatural entity that would listen to his problems and have enough power to help him solve them. He asked many questions and Dominick, sensing the emptiness in the boy, answered him. Sol felt very drawn to the Holy Mother. She seemed to be an extension of *Bubbe* Miriam, to whom his mother always prayed. Furthermore, in Sol's personal experience a mother was a source of comfort and love, while a father was often frightening and unpredictable. It all fitted together perfectly, and he effortlessly combined *Bubbe* Miriam and the Holy Mother into one comforting deity. At home, in his bed, he prayed to *Bubbe* Miriam, and when he was with Dominick he prayed to the Holy Mother. He knew they were one and the same, but instinctively he knew that his parents might not understand that, and so he never spoke about his discovery to them.

That year, he celebrated Christmas Eve with the Fusaros. Dominick gave him a New Testament and a string of rosary beads. The rest of the family gave him toys and books and games. He had never received a present before, and he was overwhelmed by the thought that these gifts had been specially purchased just for him, with no purpose but to make him happy. Sol had a sense that the New Testament and rosary beads would not be well-received at home, so he hid them away at the bottom of the El Producto and Dutch Master Cigar boxes that housed his baseball card collection.

Each night, after Helen kissed him good night and returned to the store, Sol would creep out of bed, retrieve the beads and the Bible, and read the verses Dominick had marked. Then he would ask God to help his mother with all her problems in the store, the wise-guys who scared her, the products that confused her, and the accounting of sales and deliveries that exhausted her and made her cry.

Regarding his father, he asked God to please stop him from getting so angry, and to cure the terrible rash he had all over his body. The rash was being treated by a local doctor with an assortment of creams and lotions, but it grew steadily worse until Pop Fusaro sent David to his own doctor, who realized at once that it was a nervous rash and that all the medication he had been given was making it worse. He stopped all topical medication and prescribed some mild tranquilizers. David soon showed signs of improvement, solidifying Sol's faith in the Holy Mother.

Helen and David were totally unaware of Sol's search for spiritual comfort and the route he had taken to find it. Although they were both deeply religious in their own way they had no time or energy to teach Solomon about Judaism. In their experience, Judaism was something that you grew up with, it was internalized automatically. They knew they weren't giving Sol the childhood they would have liked to give him, but they had no choice. Religion was put on hold, along with picnics at the beach, birthday parties, and all the other things they hoped to give him as soon as the terrible minute to minute pressure of avoiding bankruptcy, losing the store, and paying their debts was over.

Helen, of course, lit *Shabbat* candles every Friday night, as she had promised *Bubbe* Miriam she would. From the day she was liberated, she never once neglected to keep this promise. They also always closed the store early on Pesach so they could have a *Seder* together, and they didn't open on Rosh Hashanah and Yom Kippur. They were unaware that, since Sol was constantly surrounded by Catholics, he was not internalizing the Jewish customs as they had done. On the contrary, he witnessed these isolated rituals as peripheral activities and in no way saw them as central to his spiritual identity.

While Helen believed that she had been spared to give life to future generations of Jews—hence her determination to have children despite the five miscarriages—she had no idea that her only son had no sense of his Jewish identity at all.

Meanwhile, for David, being Jewish was an integral part of his personality. He was proud of his heritage and quick to defend it against slurs by anti-Semitic Poles around him. And as they quickly found out, David was not someone to be trifled with. However, he had always been just as quick to regain his good humor. He never remained angry for very long. This ability to bounce back from his anger made David a respected and well-liked young man.

From the moment the Nazis sealed him into a cattle-truck there had been a bubbling rage inside him. When he woke up in the morning it was there, and although the events of the day distracted him, it was there when he went to sleep at night. He was consumed with fury and frustration. In the camps, his rage had kept him strong and fighting, and at the top of any hierarchy that developed. In Germany, after the war, his anger had given him the drive to establish a successful feather business, just as his father and grandfather had done.

However, in America, where he was a no one, a *greener,* a nothing, his anger had no constructive outlet. He could not speak the language. He had no skills that were valued here. He was powerless and forced into bowing and scraping. Unexpressed, his anger knew no bounds. He tried not to unleash his fury on his family, but he was not always able to anticipate his reactions, and in the early years in the Bronx, he had often lashed out at his son.

One day, Sol had gone for a ride with a neighborhood boy, who was delivering groceries. It was an exciting ride for Sol. Juan pedaled his bicycle and Sol sat in the cart with the bread and canned food and detergent. They went all over the city and Juan pointed out the sights. The time flew and Sol did not think about the effect his three-hour disappearance might have on his parents. Juan enjoyed Sol's company and thought nothing of happily delivering him back home just as it was getting dark. They were met by a sobbing, but relieved Helen and an enraged David. Fortunately for Juan, he was able to pedal away from Mr. Pinczewski's wrath. Sol was not so lucky. He received a beating from his father that, despite Helen's attempt to separate them, left him bruised and hyperventilating with fear. When David saw what he had done, he left the apartment and went for a very long walk.

Helen lifted Sol up in her arms and hugged him to her, crooning comforting words. After a while she laid him gently on the bed, put ice on his bruises, and told him over and over again how much she loved him.

Unfortunately it wasn't long before Sol had another opportunity to feel David's wrath. His father had made him a piggy-bank, and whenever he could Sol dropped a penny or nickel into it. Sometimes David or Helen would drop in a coin too. Eventually it became extremely heavy. and it was a great source of pride and happiness to Sol. He often picked it up and rattled it around, imagining what he would do with the contents.

One evening, his parents went to a wedding, and they left him at home with a baby-sitter. When he was asleep his baby-sitter emptied the piggy-bank. A couple of days later, David picked it up and noticed how light it was. He immediately turned on Sol and accused him of using the money to buy candy for some kids who had come by the store that week. David was furious. He yelled that Sol did not understand how hard they worked for every penny and shook him so hard that it made him nauseous. Oblivious to his son's distress, David defamed him for being the most irresponsible, untrustworthy boy a father could have.

Sol tried in vain to explain that he had not touched the money. Helen attempted to intervene on his behalf, but David would not listen. Finally, she picked Sol up and carried him out of his father's reach.

A few months later, David found out that this babysitter was indeed a thief and had been stealing from other families as well. He suffered intense remorse. He was utterly dismayed that he had lost control, mistrusted his own son and abused him so horribly.

He tried his best to avoid taking his fury out on his family, but the stress of running the candy store, and the disrespect with which he was treated in that environment was overwhelming.

Most frustrating for David was that he knew from previous experience that an understanding of the local rules was essential for survival. And as hard as he tried he could not understand the complexities of this new environment. He had learned how to survive in the Polish army and Hitler's concentration camps. Helen, too, had learned the dos and don'ts of a variety of situations, but in spite of their extensive experience, they had never been in a situation quite like this. They watched carefully and tried to learn from those around them, but there were nuances they could not identify or comprehend. Here the lines between the "good guys" and the "bad guys" were not clearly drawn, and this was very different from their past experience.

David and Helen had to treat everyone as if they were "good guys." The guys coming in for coffee and a newspaper at five in the morning, and for a packet of cigarettes at midnight, were to be regarded simply as their clientele. Who they really were, what their occupations might be, and even how Helen and David were treated by them was not important. They dared not offend anyone. Worse, they had no insight into what might offend and cause their clientele to go elsewhere. So when a man asked Helen if she had numbers tattooed on her arm because she was too dumb to remember her phone number, she didn't respond. David began to show signs of responding, but with a look Helen reminded him that as much as it galled him, he had to ignore the rudeness and the insults.

They were in unfamiliar territory, weak, ignorant, and vulnerable.

They didn't understand the police either. Initially, they had been intimidated by the uniforms, badges, the sirens, but in time they overcame these fears. David asked the police for help with the many young men who loitered in the store. The police seemed willing to oblige and told the boys to leave, citing fire codes and cajoling them to move on. The boys obeyed without much of a fuss, but as soon as the police left, they all returned. Only Helen and David were surprised. No one seemed really afraid of these policemen. And the policemen seemed to accept that. It was as if they were all acting out a charade. Everyone was playing a game with rules they all understood except Helen and David. Many times a policeman would help himself to a soda or a packet of cigarettes without offering to pay for them. Neither Helen nor David ever asked them for money. Some policeman never took anything without paying. There seemed to be no distinguishable pattern.

David usually had a nap in the afternoons between two o'clock and five, and it was then that the local youths congregated in the store. They preferred to come when David was not there because he was inclined to snap and threaten them. There were those who used the store as a meeting place. They would hand over a parcel or a letter, have a few words of conversation with another customer, and leave. Sometimes they bought something, sometimes they didn't, but buying was clearly incidental. It was clear that under the Becks' control the store had been a local meeting place. Was this good for business, or bad for business? They really didn't know.

Then there was a young man who came in regularly just to make trouble. He never bought anything, but always made a point of knocking over the newspaper stand or a candy display. He would swear at Helen and accuse her of setting things up badly. The first time it happened Helen apologized profusely, but when she saw this was a game he was playing she began to ignore him. She learned to say nothing and wait until he had left to restore order. She noticed some of the other boys watching her handling the situation and saw in their eyes some grudging respect. This encouraged her to continue to ignore him, but the young troublemaker did not like being ignored.

One afternoon, when David was not around and Helen was busy with a customer, he sidled up to the waste-paper basket, threw in a lit match, and ran out of the store. One of the young men who had been watching responded instantly. He picked up the bin and took it outside where he doused it with water before it caused any damage. Helen watched this in amazement. As soon as the fire was out, the young man, whose name was Buster, left, so she never had an opportunity to thank him. She waited apprehensively for the troublemaker to come in the next day, but he didn't. In fact, he never came into the store again.

As time passed, Helen learned to distinguish between the different types. Some were merely loud and boisterous kids who had a bit of money in their pockets and felt powerful in their leather jackets and Brylcreemed hair. They just wanted somewhere to throw their weight around. Helen soon learned to deal with them and even enjoyed their antics at times.

Often they helped her carry heavy boxes or communicate with customers and vendors.

Others had more devious and destructive designs. One morning, two men came in and without bothering to ask permission, simply set up a display of shirts near the front. In response to Helen's questions, they said they would be there until all the shirts were sold, probably for the rest of the day. Helen did not know what to do. She suspected the merchandise was stolen, but was afraid to confront them.

"Don't look so worried, lady," they said. "It'll be good for you. The people who come in to buy a shirt will pick up a newspaper or a soda."

Helen was not convinced this was good for her at all. She was afraid of what might happen if a policeman showed up and caught these guys breaking the law in her store. What if they blamed David and Helen for this? They might lose their business license, or worse, be deported. Their American citizenship was very precious to them and they never took it for granted.

David decided he had to risk confronting the vendors and asking them to leave.

They just laughed and ignored him.

But neither David nor the vendors knew that there had been a witness to this interaction.

CHAPTER TWELVE

ONE OF THEIR MOST INTRIGUING customers was an impeccably groomed, quietly spoken man who came in every day to buy the newspaper and a packet of cigarettes. He was always very polite and usually addressed David and Helen by name. He had a deep, compelling voice and a measured manner of speaking. Whenever he strode into the store, all the thugs either left or became very quiet and respectful. He was obviously very important and, judging from the shiny new Cadillac he drove to the Nineteenth Hole each day, he was also very rich.

Many famous people, including Frank Sinatra and Vic Damone, were believed to frequent the Nineteenth Hole. The daytime bartender, whom they called Uncle Larry, was even rumored to be Frank Sinatra's godfather.

The day after David's unsuccessful attempt to to run the hustling shirt peddlers out of his store, the Cadillac pulled up right in front of the store, and this mysterious gentleman entered with no other goal than to speak to Helen. In no uncertain terms he told her that she should have never given the men permission to sell shirts from her store.

“The answer to them should have been no,” he said, “and that will be your answer to anyone else who asks.”

Helen explained that she and David had tried to refuse.

The man cut her off gently, “Don’t worry about that. In the future, you just tell them that I said that nobody is allowed to sell their merchandise in your store. You run a clean place here. We’re gonna keep it that way.”

Helen felt her eyes tear up. No one had talked to her in this care-taking tone since she was a young girl. She looked into this man’s face and saw strength, integrity, and for some inexplicable reason, a deep and genuine concern for her welfare.

“You’re a good man. Thank you, sir,” she said, trying to keep her breaking voice calm. To her surprise he reached for her hand, turned it over, and stretched out her arm, revealing the two sets of numbers tattooed there.

With great compassion he looked into her eyes and said, “I will allow no more ill-treatment of you or your family.”

She saw in his eyes an understanding and acceptance of the enormity of the evil she had endured.

Most people were afraid to confront the facts that were coming out about the German concentration camps. But this man was not afraid. “You have courage and heart; I have seen it. Now you must learn to live on our street,” he said.

In Poland, a man of great learning, wisdom, and spiritual power was referred to as a *Gaon.* Since this mysterious stranger had some superpower, Helen and David began referring to him by this epithet.

The *Gaon* was as good as his word. In his quiet, understated way, he taught Helen and David how to live on 86th Street.

Helen trusted him implicitly. She knew he communicated with them on a need to know basis and learned not to request or give any more information than was strictly necessary. Her life experience had taught her how to hold her tongue, and she knew that “squealing” was as unacceptable here as it had been in the camps.

The *Gaon* took care of anyone that attempted to harass them.

There was a young thug, Guido, who hung around in the store a lot. He liked to ask for an ice cream pop, take a bite, and if he didn't like it, throw it onto the clean floor. Eventually, Helen had enough of cleaning up his mess. "Guido," she said one day, "that's enough. You get out of my store and stay out, forever!"

That night, Helen waited for the newspapers to be delivered. The early editions of the *Daily News* and *Daily Mirror* usually came at about nine-thirty. Customers who came in to buy a newspaper also bought a soda, a cup of coffee, or a packet of cigarettes. By ten, when the papers weren't there, she had already lost three or four customers.

Helen called the delivery service, but they assured her that the papers had been sent to her as usual. By midnight, when the papers had still not arrived she became frantic. Her customers had all left the store disgruntled and gone somewhere else for the paper and coffee, and who knew if they'd ever come back.

She kept walking in and out of the store, checking and rechecking each nook and cranny in case they had been put in a different place on the curb. Every half hour, she called the delivery service, who kept assuring her the papers had been delivered.

Finally, Torcho, a young man she had come to like, came up to her and said, "Yo, Helen, it's two o'clock in the morning. Go to sleep. Don't bother waiting for those newspapers."

"What do you mean?" asked Helen. "Are you crazy? I gotta wait for them. David's gonna come in here at five and tell everyone we got no newspapers?"

"They not gonna come. Go to bed."

When Helen ignored him, he muttered, "Mama mia, they gonna kill me for this. They gonna bust my *kulyoonies*, but I gotta tell you."

"Tell me what?"

"You never heard this from me, right?"

"Right."

"The papers came. They delivered them same time as usual. But you was inside, and someone threw…"

"It was Guido!"

"Yea, he was pissed off at you, and he threw them in the sewer. I know you. You gonna wait all night, so that's why I'm telling you. But don't you ever say anything about me setting you wise about this. Kappish?"

Helen never told anyone that Torcho had given her this information. When the *Gaon* asked, next morning, why there were no papers, she told him that she knew Guido had thrown them into the sewer. He never asked for the source of her information. He trusted that she would never make an accusation unless she was sure of her facts. Besides, he didn't want to know. Knowledge was often a burden for him, since it required action on his part.

Guido never came into the store again, and from then on, when he walked down 86th Street, he walked on the other side of the street. Helen never asked how this came about. She merely expressed her gratitude, and the *Gaon* acknowledged her thanks with a nod.

Because Helen was so quick to learn what the *Gaon* expected of her, giving her protection was simple, and Helen and David's Sweet Shoppe was never robbed, used as a meeting place, or trashed just for the fun of it.

Helen knew with unwavering certainty that *Bubbe* Miriam had sent this man to take care of them. His wisdom about the ways of the world and his kindness and generosity were all she would see in him. If anyone tried to tell Helen or David that there were parts of the *Gaon's* life where compassion and morality were unknown, they simply would not listen. It was not their concern.

The *Gaon* also kept an eye on Solomon, who was often bullied by the neighborhood boys. He observed that when Solomon was beaten up and came home crying, his father became exasperated and his mother cleaned his wounds and wiped his tears. No one was encouraging the boy to stand up for himself.

One afternoon, he took Sol aside, bent down next to him so that they were eye to eye, and said, "You must fight back or they will have no respect for you. You are as big and as strong as they are. Hurt someone and then they will not fight with you again."

Sol balked at the thought of fighting, but the *Gaon* insisted, "Go on, go right now. I will stand here and watch as you walk down to the corner where they are. When they start taunting you, answer them. If they fight, hurt someone. If I see you are in trouble I will come and help. Go. No one should feel entitled to hurt you, Sol. Go."

Emboldened by his words and his presence, Sol swaggered off to the corner, and when the first boy pushed into him, he pushed back. Remembering the injunction to hurt someone, he swung a punch that landed on the unsuspecting boy's face. Exhilarated by the effect of his violence and the knowledge that the *Gaon* was close by, Sol taunted, "There's more where that came from. So stay out of my way."

Stunned by the shock of this response from their former victim, all three boys right away stepped back. Solomon flipped them off and swaggered back to the store. The *Gaon* was waiting for him there. "You learned something today didn't you?" Sol nodded. "I know you were scared. You're sweating and still shaking, but you did good." He ruffled Sol's hair. "Choose anything in the store, Sol, and if your mother says okay, I'll buy it for you." Sol asked for an ice cream cone and enjoyed it all the more knowing the Gaon was proud of him and that he'd never be beaten up again.

The wise guys who met to conduct business at The Nineteenth Hole were Helen's best customers. She and David were on first name terms with many of them. Before every holiday, David would remind Helen to put aside two greeting cards for each of the boys from the bar. They always bought one for their wives and one for their sweethearts, also known as coumaddas in Italian. Eventually, Helen also made a list of all the relevant birthdays and anniversaries. They relied on her to pick out the cards, but sometimes she slipped up. One day Lefty's wife told Helen, "Lefty's an idiot! I just got the same birthday card from him that I got last year. What's wrong with him? Can't he remember from one year to the next?"

After that, Helen kept a list of which cards had been sent to which women.

Sometimes, on Saturday and Sunday afternoons, Sol used to sit in the Fusaros' driveway looking out for wedding limousines. When he saw one pull up at The Nineteenth Hole, he'd run into the store and get Helen. Together they'd wait for the newlywed bride and groom to emerge from the car. Then they would "*ooh*" and "*ahh*" at the lavishly embroidered gown and the endless lacey train of the bride and the beautiful dresses of the girls in the wedding party.

These couples often stopped off at the bar for a cocktail after the ceremony at St. Bernadette's or St. Finbar's, but to Helen and Solomon they were Snow White and Prince Charming on their way to the ball. In time Helen began to recognize many of these young people, and she would go into the bar and wish them good luck.

One day, Sol ran into the store and asked Helen for permission to run an errand for one of the boys. Helen, distracted, just nodded her approval.

Sol was thrilled. He ran into the back, washed his hands, brushed his hair, and ran off happily to work. He was to get paid for his help and this made him feel grown-up and useful. Less than a minute later, he was back, looking forlorn and dreadfully disappointed. Right behind him was the *Gaon.*

"Helen, listen to me. Sol must go to school, play with his friends, and help you and David. And that is all!"

Startled, Helen took Sol's hand and looked up at the *Gaon*, who was at least a foot taller than she was. "Oh. I thought…I guess I made a mistake," she said quietly. She asked for no explanation, and he turned on his heel, not planning to give her one. Just when she thought she knew what was going on, she found out she knew nothing.

"One step on that path, and there's no going back," the *Gaon* said, almost mournfully. He knew the time had come to make Helen aware of the circumstances in which she lived. "None of you are to buy from or work with any of these wise guys. They'll bring you trouble. Do you understand?"

Not sure that she did, Helen nodded nervously. Who were these "wise guys"?

A short time after this, she began to understand better. Jerry Rosenberg, a Jewish boy who hung around at The Nineteenth Hole, said to her one day, "Hey, Helen, last night a lot of things fell off a lot of trucks. You know what I mean? Make me a list of everything you need. I can get you anything. I mean it, anything. I got connections. It's no problem. Come on! Tell me what you need. For you, for David, for the boy. It's not right that you should work so hard."

Helen laughed. "Bring me some new legs," she said. "These are tired."

Jerry turned to David. "I can get you cigarettes and stuff to sell in the store for half the price you pay now. Come on, don't you wanna make some real profit for a change?"

It was tempting, especially since Jerry was a local Jewish boy. Helen and David knew his family. But they also knew that nothing really fell off trucks. They understood that dealing with Jerry was heading down the path the *Gaon* had warned them against.

"Even his own mother knows he's trouble," Helen said with a sigh. "We can't do this."

Like many of the women who came into the store, Jerry's mother confided in Helen and shared her concerns about Jerry. One day, utterly distraught, Mrs. Rosenberg pulled Helen aside and said, "I was going to hang up the laundry. I reached into the

basket for the old sock where I keep the clothes pegs and *oy vay* Helen, there was a gun in it! A gun. Under all the dirty shirts and underwear my Jerry had hidden a gun!"

"Sha," Helen said. "Forget about it. You never saw a gun. Maybe it belonged to one of his friends, and he kept it as a favor. Maybe he didn't even know it was there." Helen poured a cup of coffee for Mrs. Rosenberg and commiserated with her on the tribulations of motherhood in this neighborhood. When she had calmed down, they hugged each other and she thanked Helen for being a good friend.

Helen's experiences in Zyberstoff, Blechammer, and Bergen-Belsen had taught her to treasure the friendship of women. The support and love she had received when she needed it and had given when she could, played a crucial role in her survival. In Brooklyn too, it was her friendships with women that gave her the strength to cope with her difficult situation.

Helen befriended two Italian Catholic women with whom she remained close the rest of her life. Marta, known as Martha, worked for the phone company. Since David opened up the store at five-thirty and usually went to sleep at about nine-thirty, Helen was in the store alone until she closed the store at two o'clock. So Martha would come to the store to keep Helen company. Josie Kopcha, who lived nearby, also dropped in most nights. Martha and Josie were usually both there by ten-thirty and most nights they ended up staying with Helen until she went to bed. Ostensibly they stayed to take care of Helen, but the truth was they all had so much fun together, they didn't want to leave.

Often the *Gaon* would see the three women in the store late at night, and he would bring in Romano's eggplant Parmesan, or that night's special from Sirocco's, or pastries from Ferrara's in Little Italy. Little Solomon would often join in these late night feasts. Although they constantly shushed him off to bed, eating inevitably took precedence over sleep. Besides, Solomon loved listening to the women talk. The three of them were much funnier than anything he saw on "I love Lucy."

Solomon knew that if he was really quiet, they might get so carried away they'd forget he was there. Then he'd curl up on the floor in a blanket and fall asleep to the sound of them chuckling, as Martha threatened to "shove a broomstick up that wise guy's ass," or Josie did hilarious impersonations of Guido. Helen jokingly gave Martha a new name, calling her Matharette. It stuck as they all got a kick out of her new nickname.

The only time the women didn't get along was when the occasional newspaper story about the latest exploits of Eleanor Roosevelt got the women talking about the late president, Franklin Delano Roosevelt.

Surprisingly, it was non-Jewish Martharette who insisted that FDR should have done more to save Jewish lives. "He sat there by his fireside, telling us all we had to fear was fear itself," complained Martharette, "while he was too afraid to do anything to help. It's because of people like him that you and David lost everybody. Our boys should have been dropping bombs on the train tracks to those concentration camps. And why couldn't your people have come here in the first place? FDR should've got rid of the quotas and allowed you all in."

Helen would not let her get away with that. "Martha, you don't know what you're talking about! Mrs. Roosevelt saved us. The British soldiers had no idea how to feed people who had been starving. After liberation, they gave us canned meat! Can you believe that? Meat for people who had been eating scraps of bread and potato skins and drinking what water they could find in rain-puddles. Our stomachs couldn't take it. Thousands died from diarrhea until Mrs. Roosevelt came to Bergen-Belsen and the other DP camps. She taught them what to give us to eat. If not for her, we would have all died."

"You always tell me that story, but what does it have to do with what FDR should have done?"

"They're good people. That's all there is to it. You want to be pissed off with somebody? I'll give you a list of people to be pissed off with."

Josie never let these disagreements go on for too long. She would interject with some risqué witticism about Mr. Roosevelt, and men in general, and they would move on. Josie had a repertoire of homilies to which she regularly resorted. She would tell the girls, "There are two sides to every story. Remember, a bell goes ding-dong." She also advised Helen, "Always respect a dog on account of its owner."

Martharette adored Coney Island, and a couple of times she managed to convince Helen to take some time off and go there with her. Martha's favorite ride was the parachute jump. Huge cables pulled two-seater parachutes up the sides of the tall towers built for the 1939 World's Fair. When it reached the top, the parachute opened and the girls came hurtling down to the ground at a terrifying speed.

Mostly, Helen was able to enjoy these outings and keep her bad memories buried, but there were bad days. Once she and Martha were in the bathroom at Nathan's where they were eating hot dogs, Martha handed Helen the bar of soap that had been put out on the sink. Helen looked at the manufacturer's logo etched into it and flashed back to the soap she had been forced to use in Blechammer concentration camp. She had completely blocked this memory from her mind. Now the image of that soap filled her brain. It was the same slim rectangular shape as this piece, and it had the letters RYF etched into it in a way that was reminiscent of this logo. RYF was "Reine Yiddishe Fet," Pure Jewish Fat. Desperately filthy prisoners had grabbed any opportunity to wash, irrespective of the circumstances. Helen now clearly remembered that she had washed herself with soap made from the corpses of her people.

She felt the room spin about her, and she grabbed onto the sink to steady herself. "Helen!" Martha cried. "What's wrong with you?"

"Nothing. I'm all right. Just dizzy." How could she put such an atrocity into words? And if she did, what would Martha think of her? She would be repelled. How would they continue through the day with this horrible truth about human evil floating in the air between them? No, she couldn't do it.

Martha wiped Helen's forehead with a wet paper towel and wisely did not press for more details.

The girls brought Helen back home but what a home it was. Helen and David had cleaned the place up as well as they could, but the tiny living space at the back of the candy store was still a disaster. They never did get the bathtub replaced, nor could they afford to have the showerhead repaired properly.

Helen developed painful boils and abscesses because she was unable to get fully clean. A wonderfully kind and sympathetic Sicilian doctor visited her regularly, but he could not cure her unless she rested her body and gave her system a chance to fight these Staph infections.

Finally, she agreed to take some time off. They would close the store one afternoon a week. The Drexlers closed their store on Tuesday afternoons, so David and Helen decided to do the same.

Soon after that Max brought some good news. He was giving up the chicken farm where he'd been living since 1953. At the urging of his wife and her family, Max had moved out of the city and bought a chicken farm near Atlantic City in Hammonton, New Jersey. Helen and David had been dismayed by this decision. They did not particularly like their sister-in-law, Anna, or her family, and they thought Max had married beneath his intellect. After all, he was always the smart one of the family. What was he doing in the stench of a chicken farm?

Once, when Sol went to visit his aunt and uncle, he was playing in the meadow with his cousin Dinah, and he fell into a pond. Max dived in and saved his life. David was extremely grateful, but Helen became reluctant to let Sol visit on his own after that.

In May of 1956, Max was delivering eggs in the city, and he came to visit his brother in the candy store.

"I have good news for you," he said. "We are selling the farm and coming back to live in the city. Enough with Hammonton and the *fashtinkenner (smelly)* chickens."

David was thrilled. He knew that if he had a partner like Max in the business, there would be no stopping them. He had learned a great deal since he opened the store and with Max's knowledge of English and a pooling of their funds they could set themselves up in a really good business. They would sell this store and the farm and buy something grand in a Jewish neighborhood where their children could go to school with other Jewish kids. They'd combine everything they had learned and all the money they'd saved, and the bad years would be over. Certainly it was time. According to the Bible, seven lean years should be followed by seven fat years, and they were greatly overdue. They drank a toast to their futures and stayed up late into the night making plans.

CHAPTER THIRTEEN

FOUR WEEKS LATER, ON June 10th, 1956, Helen sent Josie and Martha home early. It was raining hard and the thunder was deafening. She kissed her friends good-bye, brushed the last of the cake crumbs off her fingers, and went to bed herself. David was still awake.

"What are you waiting for?" she teased him.

"Nothing from you, that's for sure," he replied.

"Good," she said with a chuckle, as she seductively snuggled up next to him.

"I was thinking about how it will be when Max leaves the farm and comes to the city," David said happily. He kissed his wife's neck and she put her arms around him.

Helen had just fallen asleep when she heard the phone ringing. They had two public telephone booths in the back of the store, and occasionally people used those numbers to call them.

But not at three o'clock in the morning.

She ignored the ringing for a while, thinking it was a wrong number, but it didn't stop, so she got up and went to pick up the receiver.

"Yes," she barked into the phone.

"Helen, it's me, Paula."

Paula was Anna's sister-in-law. Helen felt her throat close and a freeze creep up her body. Why was Paula calling at this time?

"Paula? What is it? What's happened?"

"It's Max."

"Max, what about him?"

"He's…in the hospital."

"The hospital. Why? What's wrong with him?"

"He got hurt."

"Hurt? What do you mean?"

"Hurt. It means hurt."

"Okay. We're on our way. Where is the hospital?"

"No, don't go to the hospital. Come here, to Anna."

"Why would we come there if Max is in the hospital?"

"Uhm…"

Helen was out of patience. "Paula, what the hell is going on?" she demanded.

"Okay. You wanna know, I'll tell you. He was struck by lightning and he's dead."

Helen yelled into the phone, "That's not true."

Now Paula was weeping. "It's true. He was out in the storm, covering up the chickens, and he got hit."

"NO! NO! NO!" Helen tried to block out the meaning of Paula's words with her screams.

This woke David and Sol, who both rushed up to see what was happening. "Helen, what is it?" David yelled. His face had lost all color. He had never seen Helen react like this to anything.

She just stood with the phone in her hand screaming, "NO! NO! NO!"

Helen couldn't speak at all. She couldn't tell David what had happened. She could not put this into words. Perhaps, she also knew that once David knew what had happened, he would need her help and her time for expressing her pain would end.

By this time, her screams had been heard in the Nineteenth Hole and Philidelis. Rocky and Charlie Chip came to see what was happening. They all kept asking, "What happened? What happened?" But she couldn't speak.

Finally, Rocky sent one of the boys to get her some brandy. David held it to her lips. She took a few sips and calmed down a little, but she still could not bear to tell David what had happened. She looked at him and shook her head.

"Who?" he insisted. "Just tell me who?"

"Max," she whispered. Once she had said the name, the rest followed. "Max was struck by lightning. He was out in the storm, with the chickens. He...he..."

David said nothing. He just turned away and banged his forehead into the wall. Once, twice, three times, four times.

No one spoke.

The only sound was David's head connecting with the wall in a steady rhythm. Five times, six.

This scared Sol more than his mother's screaming and he threw himself against his father's leg. "Stop, Dad. Please stop."

Rocky took David's arm. "I'll drive you there. Let's go."

David nodded. What did Paula know? Max was probably just hurt, stunned, not dead. He went over to the refrigerator and took out the $2000 he had stowed there for an emergency. It was all the money he had in the world, but if Max needed something he could have it all. Helen, David, and Sol threw on some clothes, Sol grabbed his teddy bear and his rosary beads, and the three of them got into Rocky's car. "Stay as long as you need," said Charlie. "We'll take care of the store."

They got to the farm just as dawn was breaking. It was still raining and only scattered patches of light succeeded in breaking through the dark clouds. Anna, Dinah, some neighbors, and a few relatives were in the house, and Helen and Sol went in to join them.

David ran outside to the barn where Max's body had been left after it was dragged in from the storm. He threw himself onto the ground alongside his brother's lifeless body and begged him to wake up. "Please!" he cried. "Please don't die. Not now. How could you live through all that and then die like this?"

Anna's brother came up behind David and gently helped him to his feet. "He died instantly," he said. "The doctor said the lightning went straight through his heart. At least he didn't suffer."

David said nothing. The two of them carried Max into the house.

The memorial service was held in a chapel in Brooklyn. The tragic news had traveled quickly, and many survivors who knew Max made their way to the I.J. Morris funeral parlor on Flatbush Avenue. Afterwards, they all drove to the New Jersey cemetery. It was, for many, the first loss they had experienced since the end of the war, and Max's sudden death triggered deeply buried emotions that had been blocked and locked away behind thick walls of determination to forget.

Now memories of the terrible losses they had all suffered burst out of the confines in which they had been repressed for so long. The air was filled with weeping and the tangible presence of the friends and family members whose lives had been abruptly terminated by the Nazis.

Helen and David could not contain their pain. They howled out their grief.

Sol let go of his mother's hand and ran to the back of the mourners. There he cowered, bent over double, pressing his hands against his eyes and ears to block out the anguish and agony that surrounded him.

Finally, the strains of the *Kaddish* faded into the New Jersey countryside and the mourners expressed their heartfelt condolences. They vowed to get together soon under happier circumstances and offered to help any way they could.

Rocky drove Helen, David and Sol back home. They didn't go inside. David went over to the Nineteenth Hole and asked Larry, the daytime bartender, for a basin of water. Helen, David, and Sol washed their hands. In accordance with Jewish custom this had to be done after a funeral before the mourners could enter their home.

Sol was exhausted, bewildered, and relieved to be back home. He hoped life would get back to normal. However, to his chagrin, things became even stranger. His mother now covered the cracked bathroom mirror with a towel and instead of going into the store, she and his father took off their shoes and sat down on the floor. His father had torn his shirt at the funeral, and now in his torn shirt he sat weeping and chanting in Hebrew, a language Sol did not understand. He watched, afraid to approach, as his father rocked back and forth weeping and praying.

Once *shiva,* the traditional Jewish seven days of mourning, was over, Helen knew she had to take care of the business and her family. With the help of her friends, her faith, and her late night monologues with *Bubbe* Miriam, Helen went back to work, but David could not overcome his utter despair. The pain of this unexpected, inexplicable loss of his only surviving family member was unbearable. His mind and heart shut down in the face of it. He sank into a deep and severe depression. Often he woke up at night, confused and disoriented, wondering why he felt such a deep sadness. On the edge of sleep, he would for a few minutes, remain mercifully unaware of the source of the heaviness inside him.

Then, he would remember.

He'd wake Helen. "How could God, blessed be his name, do this? Why? How much suffering does He want?"

"Shhh," Helen whispered tenderly. "Shhh. Only in heaven will we know why."

"But why after we lost everyone did He take my brother? Why? Why? Why?"

Pop Fusaro, seeing David's pain etched on his face, sent him to see his personal physician, who gave David high doses of antidepressant medication. It helped somewhat, but the side effect of such a high dosage was that David could hardly stay awake. He barely helped around the store and slept most of the day.

With David diminished and unable to carry his share of the work load, though she felt bad about it, Helen had to ask for even more help from her young son. Every day, when he got back from school, he worked in the store. Weekends weren't spent playing stickball or any of the other usual pastimes of an eight-year-old American boy. Instead, Sol now carried the heavy soda crates back and forth, from the basement where they were stored, to the Coca-Cola box upstairs, where they were cooled in ice water.

Soon inventory also became his responsibility. He checked the orders, the deliveries, and the payments.

To make things more difficult, a soccer team that played on the field across the road, rented out the basement and used it as a locker room. This meant Sol had to make his way around the large noisy men who nicknamed him "Bottles" because he was always carrying bottles of soda from the basement to the store, and carrying the empty bottles back down to the basement.

One steamy summer day when the city streets got so hot it seemed the asphalt would melt, a tall, robust, black woman wearing the gaudiest hat Helen had ever seen, came in and asked if she could work once or twice a week as a cleaning lady. Flossie, who had a cheerful rich Southern voice and a broad smile, couldn't have chosen a better moment to offer her services. Helen's boils and varicose veins were giving her excruciating pains, and she was sorely tempted to hire her. She thought how wonderful it would be if on Tuesday afternoons, when they closed the store, Flossie could come in and clean up the place.

While she was talking to Flossie, Helen noticed some customers staring at her. "What's wrong with them? Why are they looking at you like that?" asked Helen, with her usual directness.

Flossie roared with laughter, and in her strong Southern drawl she exclaimed, "Well, I do declare.

Miz Helen, you are a wonder. You really don't know. It's because I'm colored." There was no surer way she could have secured her employment. After what she had been through, Helen would tolerate no prejudice. She had experienced first-hand the devastation that prejudice and hatred could cause.

There was one thing that worried Helen about hiring Flossie, and that was her bulk. She must have weighed close to four hundred pounds. How would she get around in the cramped confines of the candy store? She decided however that if Flossie thought she could manage, then she probably could.

As it happened, Flossie's size did cause them some embarrassing moments. On one memorable occasion, she needed help extricating herself from the bathroom. Flossie, Helen, and Sol pushed and pulled to no avail. Eventually the fire department had to come to the store and take the door frame apart so Flossie could get out.

One Tuesday afternoon, Helen and David closed the store and while Flossie cleaned, they took Sol out for a treat—Chinese dinner, then a movie at the RKO grand, and some delicious baked goods from Ebingers, a famous German bakery near the movie theater.

They returned home as the streetlamps began to come on and found Flossie standing outside the store waiting for them. Surprised to see her there so late, Helen rushed up to her and asked what was wrong. Had the store been robbed? Refusing to say a word, Flossie took Helen inside and closed the door. Then she started to cry. "Oh Miz Helen, Miz Helen. I didn't know what to do. I found a gun. It was lying right there behind them boxes. I moved them away to sweep the floor and there it was."

Helen sighed with relief and gave Flossie a glass of water and a napkin to wipe her sweaty brow. She reassured her that there was no problem and told her to put the gun and the boxes back exactly where she found them. After Flossie left, Helen went next door to The Nineteenth Hole. She was not as calm as she had pretended to be, but she was confident someone there would tell her what to do.

There she found Pete, a local businessman, sitting alone at the bar. She went up to him and, keeping her voice low, explained what had happened and what she had done about it. He nodded and, speaking just as quietly, said, "You did just the right thing. Just forget you ever saw it. I think that very soon, it will be gone." The following week, when Flossie came to clean the store, she gingerly peeked behind the boxes, and the gun was gone. No one ever mentioned it again.

In time, Helen and Flossie developed a deep understanding and respect for each other. Flossie often came early and stayed late, helping Helen with all sorts of chores. Sometimes she joined in the late night sessions with Martha and Josie. The three of them helped Helen as much as they could and made sure she was never alone for very long. Martha believed that friendship and laughter were the best cure for stress and exhaustion, and she made sure Helen had plenty of both.

Occasionally, the three friends would go into New York City to see the latest movies. Helen and Josie would take the bus and the subway, and Martha would come straight from work and meet them there. The first time any of them went to the Roxy Theater, it was to see *Imitation of Life* with Lana Turner. Helen dressed up for the occasion, wearing a bright blue hat that was as big and bold as anything Flossie wore. The girls met in the lobby and walked up the sumptuous carpeted staircase together. On the first landing, there was a large classical statue of a discus thrower. He was naked, and each detail of his anatomy was clearly defined. Martha let out a whoop when she saw the sculpture, and at the top of her voice exclaimed, “My God. Would you believe the *cojones* on this guy? Come here, we gotta measure them.” Other moviegoers watched in bemusement as Martha used her thumb and forefinger to measure the genitals of the marble hero. Helen and Josie started to giggle, calmly at first, but soon they were laughing so hard they had to sit down. There they sat, all three of them, on the crimson, carpeted staircase hanging onto the tasseled, golden handrails for support and laughing so much they could not move. Each time they were about to regain their composure, one of them would say something about size or length, which would set them all off again. Finally, they pulled themselves to their feet and went in to see the movie.

However, before the movie was halfway through Josie and Martha realized it had been a bad choice. The film told the story of a black daughter, who passed for white, and its undertones of racial prejudice affected Helen deeply. It hit too close to home. When the movie was over, she remained in her seat, sobbing, until an usher politely asked them to leave. Martha and Josie helped Helen to her feet and escorted her to the ladies’ room. As she walked in, a woman chuckled at her.

"What, you heard about us and the *cojones?*" asked Helen.

"*Cojones*? Oh, you mean the guy in the lobby? No, what happened to him? But before you tell me, look in the mirror."

Helen turned to the mirror and saw that her cheeks and forehead were streaked with blue. The tears and perspiration had caused the blue dye from her hat to run down her forehead and onto her cheeks. Josie and Martha came up behind her, saw Helen's blue streaked face, and the three of them burst out laughing again.

Now Helen became quite hysterical. The emotional ups and downs of the day overwhelmed her. She sat on the floor of the bathroom laughing, crying, blowing her nose, and wetting her pants until finally she was all laughed and cried out enough to go back home to David and Solomon.

Towards the beginning of his third grade year, Sol and Helen were having dinner when he made an unexpected announcement. "I need to start going to confession and catechism or I won't be able to take my communion," he said, with a serious look on his young face. For just a moment, she thought he might be joking, but when she saw how anxiously he was waiting for an answer, she realized something was very wrong.

"What do you mean, Sol? You're Jewish," she said gently.

"But I want to take communion. All the kids are doing it, so why can't I?"

"Gottenu," muttered Helen. She was flabbergasted but said nothing to her son. Sol had never asked for anything, yet here he was looking at her with those big eyes, asking to participate in a Catholic mass. Helen suddenly understood that Solomon had no sense of being Jewish. She and David had been so busy struggling to eke out a living in the store that they hadn't had the time to create a Jewish home for their only son. He had not been exposed to Judaism and his innate spirituality sought an outlet.

Communion! Confession! Helen knew she had to get Sol into a Jewish environment as soon as possible and redirect this longing in the right direction.

She went into the store, waited impatiently until David finished with the customer he was serving and announced, "Sol must go to the yeshiva." In response to his puzzled look she blurted out, "He just asked to take communion!"

All that night, Helen worried about her son's situation. Where would she find a Yeshiva? She knew no Jewish people in this neighborhood. Who could she ask? She decided to take the bus to the kosher butcher in Bensonhurst; he would know.

Then there was the problem of tuition. How would she pay? Public school was free. But here in the *Goldenna medina,* she would have to pay for a Jewish education.

The next morning, the butcher directed her to Yeshiva Ohel Moshe, which required another bus ride across town to 79th and Bay Parkway. Helen was ushered in to see Rabbi Leon Machlis, who told her he was delighted to meet her, that he would love to have her son in his school, and that it would cost $55.00 a month plus $10.00 a month for the lunch program.

"Wait, Rabbi, you don't understand," interrupted Helen, shocked by these numbers. "My husband and I are both Holocaust survivors. We have a small candy store in Bay Ridge and we live in the back of the store. To tell the truth, I can't afford private education for my son, and I should leave him in public school, but there are no Jewish children where we live and yesterday he asked when he is going to have a communion! So you see, Rabbi, he must come to the Yeshiva."

“Yes, I agree, he should be in Yeshiva, and I will be happy to take him, but the cost is $55.00 a month plus $10.00 for the lunch program,” repeated the Rabbi.

“Rabbi,” Helen said emphatically, “I just told you, I cannot afford that.”

“Well, Mrs. Pinczewski, I am sorry to hear that because I would really have liked to have your son.”

She stared at him, unable to believe her ears. Didn’t he care at all? Rabbi Machlis began shuffling through his papers to indicate the meeting was over.

“Are you refusing to accept my son?” she asked indignantly. “I came in here. I told you I’m a survivor who’s struggling to make a living, whose son wants to take communion, and you refuse to take him. You turn your face away from me and say if I can’t pay fifty-five dollars a month, then I survived Hitler to see my son become a Catholic!”

The Rabbi shrugged.

Helen stood up, shaking with anger. “Very well, if that’s how it is, people should know. In my store, I have everybody coming in. Lawyers, newspaper reporters, and everything. I will tell them about you. I’ll ask Lenny to put in the paper that Rabbi Leon Machlis doesn’t care if the son of survivors of Buchenwald and Bergen-Belsen becomes a Catholic.”

Helen turned on her heel and strode toward the door.

The Rabbi realized that this was a woman who was not to be trifled with; she would indeed do as she threatened. “Wait a minute,” he said, “don’t get all upset. Let’s talk about this.”

Helen hid the shudder of relief that went through her, and they did talk and came to a compromise. They settled on $25.00 a month plus lunch money. This was still going to be a great burden for Helen and David, but at least it was possible.

So, in the middle of the third grade, Sol transferred from PS 229 to Yeshiva Ohel Moshe. Each morning, he left the house wearing his *yarmulke* and endured the taunts and jeers of the other kids. Sol took two buses to get to the Yeshiva, and in the beginning, he hid his *tzitis* under his shirt.

Eventually, under the guidance of Rabbi Suberry, he gradually shifted his spiritual allegiance from the Virgin Mary to the Torah and began to wear his *tzitis* with pride. Now the rosary beads and the New Testament posed a dilemma for Sol. He no longer had any need for them, but he didn’t know what to do with them. He couldn’t hide them in his room; his mother might find them when she was cleaning. He certainly couldn’t throw them away; he knew that the beads were spiritual objects that had given him great solace when he needed it. Finally, he came up with a solution. He would leave them on the bus. One of the bus stops on his route to school was directly outside a church. Many passengers got on and off the bus there.

One morning, Sol took the beads with him and left them on the bus, hoping that a Catholic child would find them and put them to good use. He never told his mother that Dominic had given him the beads. She had an enormous capacity for enjoying herself, and was usually able to see the funny side of anything, but he did not think she would be able to laugh at how close he had come to becoming a Catholic.

Indeed, Helen did have a talent for taking the events of her life and retelling them in a way that provided endless amusement for herself and her audience. One day, when the Yeshiva called asking her to pick up Sol from school, she made the girls howl with laughter. "Oy, have I got a story for you," she said when they came in. "Today I walked down Bay Parkway showing everyone my underwear!"

"Wait!" said Josie. "This is gonna be a good one. I need a cup of coffee. Anybody else want?"

"Forget the coffee, Josie," said Martha, "I wanna hear this now."

"So okay. She can start talking. I'm listening."

“Well, I had to go and get Sol from school today because they called and said he had a fever. So I straight away left the store and took the bus. You know how I have to take two buses to get there and transfer at Bay Parkway. Anyway, as I’m getting off on Bay Parkway, a lady stands on the hem of my skirt. Of course, I don’t notice this at the time, so I keep walking. So you get the picture? She’s standing on my skirt and I’m walking away from her? The next thing, my skirt ripped open, and there I am, standing in the middle of Bay Parkway in my stockings. When I see what’s happened I push her away, grab the skirt, and try to wrap it around my waist. I was so embarrassed I thought I would die. Luckily, there was a clothes store nearby. I rushed in and grabbed the first assistant I saw. ‘Do you have a skirt for me? Size 16?’ I ask her. She looks at me, sees straight away that it’s an emergency, and brings me the first skirt she finds. I put it on, pay her, and run back to catch the next bus.

“When I get on the bus, everyone is looking at me funny. I think they must have seen what happened, or somebody told them already, so I just stare outta the window till I can get off the bus.

“Then when I get to the school I go into the office, and straight away the secretary starts laughing.

‘What?’ I ask her. ‘You also already heard what happened to me on Bay Parkway?’

"‘Bay Parkway? No.’ says the school secretary, ‘but you have half a dozen price tags and labels on the skirt you’re wearing.’

“So then I understood. That’s why they were all looking at me on the bus.”

By this time Josie and Martha were laughing so hard they couldn’t breathe. Helen was laughing too. “They probably thought I stole the dress,” she guffawed. “It wouldn’t be the first time people thought I stole something. In Germany, after the war, they also thought I was a thief. Did I ever tell you about what happened to me? How I was arrested for stealing American cigarettes? If it wouldn’t have been for David and a drunk army judge, I don’t know what would have happened to me.”

Just as Helen had omitted from her narrative how distressed she had been about the expense of having to buy a new skirt on Bay Parkway, so she said nothing about the terror she had felt in Hof at the possibility of being incarcerated in a German prison. Instead, she told them about the furious judge, dragged from a rendezvous with a buxom young *fraulein,* drunkenly busting into the prison in his jeep and shooting bullets into the wall until she was released.

Martha, Josie, and Helen had an unspoken agreement that they got together to be amusing, to make light of their troubles. They could all fill in for themselves the darker side of each other's stories. They preferred to laugh rather than cry together. However, when they looked into each other's eyes they saw the compassion they needed from each other. They were women, wives, mothers and they understood each other. At the same time Martha and Josie knew that some parts of Helen's experience were beyond their comprehension. They hoped their love and laughter could help to heal those hurts too.

CHAPTER FOURTEEN

THAT SUMMER, SOLOMON CELEBRATED his eighth birthday. He had been counting the days since the afternoon in November when his father promised to buy him a portable radio as a birthday present.

From the moment David handed it to him with the stern admonition to look after it, it was always with him. It was his best friend and his permanent companion. He could listen to the music his peers talked about, but even more important, he could listen to all the baseball games. Sol had become an avid Yankee fan while living in the Bronx and despite his move to Brooklyn, he had remained loyal to his team. This had not been easy, especially when, in the 1955 World Series, The Yankees were beaten by the Brooklyn Dodgers. It took a lot of courage to continue being the only Yankee supporter in the neighborhood. In 1956, it seemed that Sol's dogged determination not to be fickle might pay off. The

Yankees were riding high, and Sol had no doubt his team would win the World Series this time.

When Sol got home from Yeshiva and went into the store to work, he no longer felt sad and alone. His mentors, Bob Turley, Roger Maris, Moose Skowron, Don Larson, and of course Mickey Mantle were there with him. The night Mickey Mantle won the Triple Crown, Sol was so excited that they could not get him to bed. He wanted his mother to understand how important this was and he called on Martha and Josie to help him convince her that baseball was to be taken seriously. He told Helen everything he had read about Mickey Mantle in the newspapers and magazines in the store, and everything he had heard from customers who had seen him play.

He also sang Paul Anka's new song, "Goody, Goody" for the girls. He knew all the words, and he held a Coke bottle upside down in his hand as if it were a microphone. Now that he could listen to the same music as other kids his age, he found it a route to becoming one of them, to feeling he belonged. At the turn of a knob, he had Big Bopper, Dion and the Belmonts, and Paul Anka filling his world with pop music and making him feel like a regular American kid.

One day, Sol was left alone in the store to handle customers for a few minutes while his father rested. As it happened the store was busy. Sol was making an ice cream cone and an egg-crème for two waiting customers, a third strode up to him and brusquely demanded a pack of Lucky Strike. Afraid to ask the man to wait, Sol blindly reached up behind him for the cigarettes. As he groped for the box in the display above his head, he knocked the radio off its perch on the shelf. He made a grab for it, but it was too late. Horrified, he watched the radio hit the ground and shatter into a multitude of pieces that bounced and ricocheted all over the floor. Sol grabbed wildly at the pieces and tried desperately to put them back together. Then, he sat down on the floor and sobbed his heart out.

David, who had been resting in the back, came to see what all the noise was about. The sight of the waiting customers and the broken radio, together with the sound of Sol wailing was beyond David's tolerance. He lifted his son to his feet by his shirt collar and yelled into his face. "How could you do this, you clumsy boy? Why don't you watch what you're doing? You don't deserve to have a radio, if you don't know how to take care of it." He put him down on the ground and turned to help his customers.

Sol cradled the broken pieces in his lap and sobbed his heart out. Helen, who had been outside, walked in through the back door just as the *Gaon* came in from the street. His eyes met Helen's as they both took in the scene. Hardly missing a beat, he walked up to Helen and asked politely if she and David would allow him to take Sol to get a new radio. Helen gratefully nodded her assent.

The *Gaon* took Sol by the hand and they walked out to his car. They drove to 86th street and 18th Avenue and went into to Skelzo's Radio Store. There the *Gaon* said, "Sol, pick out another radio."

Sol didn't move. Mourning the loss of all that portable radio meant to him, he was totally unable to understand that someone was actually going to replace it so soon. His best hope was that he would be able to get another one for his next birthday.

The *Gaon* tapped his shoulder."Sol, this is a radio store. Go, pick out a radio. I'm going to buy it for you."

"Now?"

The *Gaon* nodded and the look of gratitude Sol threw him made the clerk smile.

"Don't you have a nice uncle?" she said.

Sol picked out a radio, but it was not until later when he had put in a battery, and turned it on that he really understood the traumatic event was over and he had his music and his Yankees back again.

Solomon's enthusiasm for baseball and the Yankees was so infectious that Helen and David finally became Yankee fans too. They were all listening when Don Larson pitched a perfect game in the World Series, twenty-seven batters up and twenty-seven batters out. They all heard the Yankees defeat the Brooklyn Dodgers to win the World Series and laughed in gleeful revenge at the Dodger fans who had written anti-Yankee slogans on a huge dummy they hung from a telephone pole outside the store.

As time went on Helen became something of a personality in the neighborhood. People knew and liked her. She achieved some standing and was usually treated with respect. Those who crossed her usually regretted it. There was the time Jimmy Cucho was looking for a job, and he arranged for prospective employers to call him at the store. On days when he was expecting a call, he paced up and down, anxiously waiting for the phone to ring. Towards mid-afternoon, he came over to Helen and said, "Listen, I gotta get outta here. I'll be down the block at the gas station. If someone calls for me just ask them to hold on and come and get me."

Helen agreed. The store wasn't busy and Jimmy was always very obliging when she needed help. The problem was that when she went to look for him, he was nowhere to be found. She tried to delay the caller as long as she could, but eventually she had no choice but to ask the prospective employer to call back. When Jimmy returned she told him what happened, and he went ballistic. He screamed at her, "You jackass! You stupid bitch, I waited all day for that call. I needed that job. How could you do this to me?" He screamed and shouted and cursed until Helen was forced to ask him to leave. This infuriated him even more and he came right up to her and continued yelling into her face.

She stepped back and commanded him to get out of the store. When he just continued yelling insults at her she lost control and slapped him across the face. Seeing the dangerous way his eyes glinted at her, she picked up a Coke bottle and hissed, "If you don't get out right now I will break this over your head." By now they had drawn quite an audience, and the boys were laughing and yelling encouragement at her. Jimmy turned on his heel and stormed out.

Bumping into Torcho at the door, he said, "Did you see that crazy woman? She hit me."

"Really?" said Torcho with a smirk. "I didn't see anything." He turned around to the other guys. "Did any of you see Helen hit him?" They all shook their heads.

"Sweet old Helen? No, never," said Danny, laughing so much he could barely talk. Helen's angry voice followed Jimmy down the street, "Don't ever, ever come back into my store. I never want to see you again!"

Jimmy stayed away for almost six months but, on Christmas Eve, he tentatively knocked on the door and said, "Heh, Helen. I'm really sorry about what happened. It's Christmas and I want to make peace with you and wish you a Merry Christmas."

Helen, who had forgiven him long before, welcomed him back to the fold. She was surprised and flattered that he cared enough to apologize. Martha and Josie were not surprised. Helen was a force to be reckoned with on 86th street.

Rosh Hashanah that year fell in the middle of a sizzling heat wave. One of the salesmen who came into the shop a few days before the holiday, suggested they go to the Catskills instead of the local temple. "Go! Get away," he urged. "You need a vacation, and the boy could do with some country air."

The morning before Rosh Hashanah, The Pinczewskis closed the store at eleven o'clock, packed up the old car they had bought from Anna, after Max died, and set off to The Highland Country Club in the Catskills, an area affectionately called the Borscht Belt. Finally, after many stops because the car was overheating, or the gears were jamming, they found themselves in the mountains.

The resort was heaven. A bath for Helen, a real bed for Solomon, and no customers to contend with. There was fresh air and leisurely relaxation. Solomon discovered his father could be funny and his mother could sit still.

The peace was shattered when, on Sunday morning, Josie came bursting into their room and said, with no preamble, "You stupid sons of bitches! You didn't lock up the store before you went. You left the place wide-open. Give me the keys so we can lock up for you!"

"Oh my God." David was pale with shock. "The bastards must have cleaned us out!"

Josie laughed. "Oh no. Nobody is going anywhere near your stuff. Your friend has two guys in the front, and two guys at the back and no-one dares even look into the store."

David could not believe this was possible, but Josie assured him that the *Gaon* had his people watching the place night and day and they would be there until she got back with the keys.

David wanted to leave right away and go back with Josie, but Helen refused. Sure enough when they got back everything was just as they had left it. In fact, in all the years they had the candy store, nothing, not even a packet of cigarettes was ever stolen from them.

One evening when David had already gone to sleep and Josie and Martha still hadn't gotten to the store for their nightly get-together, Freddie, a wannabe gangster from the neighborhood, came into the store in a rage. "Helen, give me the Gaon's phone number."

Helen said, "I don't have his phone number."

Freddie yelled, "You're full of shit! You know it. And if you don't give it to me, I'll tear your store apart."

Helen crossed her arms. "Go ahead. I'm not afraid of you. I have faced far worse threats in my life."

Freddie then calmed down and asked Helen to cash a check for him. David had cashed checks for him in the past, so Helen asked him for how much.

"Twenty-five dollars."

"The most I can do is fifteen."

Freddie agreed. She took the check he wrote out and gave him fifteen dollars, and he left. Shortly later Martha and Josie came into the store for their nightly get-together and Helen told them about Freddie.

Josie frowned. "Helen, Freddie is a dangerous guy who can fly off the handle very easily. You must be very careful around him. He has beaten up many people for no reason. He wears brass knuckles. Tell David to be careful too."

Helen did not have to be careful about Freddie for very long.

The following morning the phone rang inside one of the two pay phone booths that were at the back of the store. Helen went to answer while David took care of customers. She got to the phone after numerous rings.

It was Josie. "Guess what?"

Helen laughed. "Josie, what are you doing up so early?"

Josie chuckled. "You don't have to worry about Freddie anymore."

"What do you mean?"

"Freddie was found dead in front of the police station early this morning."

"He was? So, do you think the bank will accept the check I cashed for him last night?"

"Take it to the bank today and it should be okay."

A few days later, two homicide detectives came into the store and asked David questions about Freddie. They wanted to know who cashed his check and had other questions regarding the homicide investigation.

David had the story on the front page of *The Daily News*. "You need to talk to my wife. She cashed Freddie's check. I'll get her."

He found Helen packing shelves in the back of the store. "There are two detectives who want to ask you some questions about the night Freddie was killed." He took her arm. "Be very careful."

Helen brushed him off." I know what to do."

The detectives asked all kinds of questions about Freddie, his family, how well she knew him, and who his friends and enemies were. Helen shook her head. "I don't know anything about what you are asking."

The detective became impatient. "Lady, this is a homicide investigation, and if you don't cooperate with us we will have to take you down to police headquarters for questioning." "But I don't know anything," she said. "He asked me to cash a check and I did it. That's all I know."

Eventually they left, but they were back the next day and insisted she go with them to the police station for questioning. She told David not to worry and reminded him that she had been through far worse situations.

Helen sat in the back of the police car, telling herself she had done nothing wrong and everything would be okay. The detectives led her to a semi dark room with a chair at the far end. They asked her to be seated. The detectives stood a few feet away from her and shone a light on her. To break the silence Helen said, "If you put a few more windows in here, you wouldn't need to shine such bright lights at me."

They asked about the night Freddie came into the store. They asked about the check she cashed. They asked who else was in the store when Freddie came in.

Helen remained very calm. "I don't keep track of every customer who comes into my store. I am just happy that they come and that they buy things, so we can make a living."

They wanted to know what Freddie looked like that night. Helen made them laugh when she said, "He was dressed to kill! With a fedora hat!"

The lead detective didn't laugh. "If you don't cooperate with us we can lock you up," he said.

"You know what," Helen said, "do me a favor and lock me up. I work twelve hours a day and need some rest. Please go ahead and lock me up so I can get some sleep."

The detective stared at her for a while, then he sighed and shook his head. "I give up."

That evening when Martha and Josie came in for their nightly chat, Helen was waiting. "Did you hear about my trip to the police station today?"

Josie and Martha made themselves comfortable. They could tell from the look on her face that this was going to be a good story. And it was.

CHAPTER FIFTEEN

AS THEY APPROACHED THE summer of 1959, Helen felt for the first time in twenty years that her life was becoming normalized. She found whole days went by without her feeling anxious about the next one. The store was paying for itself, most of the debts that upset David so much had been taken care of, and he too was starting to meet the morning with anticipation rather than apprehension.

Sol was happy too. He had settled into the Yeshiva, liked the kids and his teachers, and especially loved participating in the Malava Malkas organized by Mrs. Machlis. Indeed, she regarded him as one of her star performers. He still had his boyish, soprano voice and had developed a smooth, confident manner that made her usually select him to be Master of Ceremonies for these shows.

Although Helen herself had not been able to sing a note since she was caught singing by an SS guard in the kitchen at Blechammer, she loved listening to Sol.

Josie and Martha often came to listen to him too, and cheer him on as he conducted himself with great aplomb. When his class was invited to perform for the radio station WEVD, Mrs. Machlis selected Sol to be the narrator for the group of Yeshivah boys and girls singing Hebrew songs and congratulating JFK on his election.

It was to be on a Sunday morning in December, but the snow storm that day led Sol to believe it would be canceled. He was fast asleep when the phone rang and Mrs. Machlis asked where he was. Helen rushed to wake Sol up and hurried him over to the Yeshivah to get him on the bus that would get to the studio for the radio show. Mrs. Machlis almost had a coronary but Sol got to the school in time. From there it was a long ride to Queens where Tzvee Schooler, the moderator on WEVD, was waiting and they performed for the radio audience.

Everyone in the neighborhood heard Sol on the radio. Helen called the radio station requesting a recording of the broadcast and after many calls and effort was able to get a reel to reel tape of the broadcast.

LISTEN TO THE BROADCAST HERE

When it was time to sell raffle tickets, the customers in the store, the Gaon and his associates,

Josie and Martha all showed their support for Sol. And when the Yeshiva had fundraisers Mrs. Machlis noticed the unusual and inexplicable number of unpronounceable Italian names that appeared on the stubs Sol gave her. Her only response to this phenomenon was to raise her eyebrows and remember that God moved in mysterious ways. And who was she to complain.

Sol's class had the opportunity to have an audience with the *Rebbe* of the Chabad Movement, Rabbi Schneerson. Meeting this knowledgeable charismatic man affected Sol deeply and enhanced his already strong feeling towards his faith.

One thing that did worry Helen at this time was that Frances Drexler seemed to be looking older. She tired easily and her eyes had lost their sparkle. When she asked Frances about this, Frances mumbled something about the flu, but Helen knew her friend too well to accept this explanation.

She decided to keep a close eye on her.

The Pinczewskis and the Drexlers spent most Tuesday afternoons together. Solomon and Charlie Drexler were about the same age and kept each other occupied. One afternoon when Frances was giving the boys a snack, Helen asked Harry if he had noticed that Frances had lost a great deal of weight. He sighed and admitted that they were very worried and had made an appointment with a specialist.

Helen waited anxiously for the results of the medical investigation and prayed to *Bubbe* Miriam to keep Frances well. She felt that after losing two children during the war, Harry and Frances deserved to see Charles grow to manhood. However, this was not to be. The tests revealed that Frances had leukemia. Devastated, Helen prayed to *Bubbe* Miriam to intervene on the *Chucha's* behalf, if not to cure her then at least to give her some more time with her son.

Every time she hung up the phone with Frances, Helen was overcome with weakness and sympathy pains. She felt as if she were going through the illness with her friend. Later Helen started showing symptoms herself. She threw up her breakfast every morning and something strange was happening to the shape of her stomach. She began to imagine that she had cancer too. Perhaps they had both been exposed to carcinogens in the camps. She became convinced that there was a malignant tumor growing in her belly.

For a long time, she tried to hide her fears from David, but eventually she could no longer disguise her nausea and exhaustion. David told her to go and see Dr. Oliver immediately. Always direct, the trembling Helen walked into the doctor's office and said, "I hope you can help me because I have a stomach tumor and I can't die because I have to take care of David and Sol and Charlie."

"Oh," said the doctor, "so you know what you have. Why are you here then?"

"So you can cure me."

The doctor examined her, smiling to himself as his knowing hands detected the beginning of a new life. "Helen," he said, "I don't think you would want me to cure you of this. You're pregnant, probably close to twelve weeks."

The doctors in Germany had told Helen that she could never have children. Her first born, Sol, was considered a miracle baby. She had persevered through five miscarriages to have him, and justifiably assumed another child was out of the question.

"Dr. Oliver, you wouldn't kid me about something like this, would you?"

He shook his head, and Helen began to cry. "She promised I would have children. My Bubbe, she promised. She said children, not a child, children, but I didn't believe, and now it's true." She sat up. Tears dripped from her eyes as she stroked her belly. "I'm pregnant. I'm gonna have another baby." Helen wiped her eyes. "Thank you, Doctor, thank you."

"I don't think it's me you should thank for this."

"No, I know, I mean thanks for giving me the news." She laughed. "I'm pregnant. I'm gonna have a baby. It's unbelievable!" She hugged the doctor and the nurse and utterly exhilarated she rushed back to the store to tell everyone the wonderful news.

Once Helen and David got used to the idea, plans had to be made. There was no room for another child in the back of the candy store and anyway they could now afford to move to a regular apartment. Helen had kept in contact with Blame, whose family had hidden Max from the Nazis and given David's whole family shelter after the Germans destroyed their home. Blame now suggested the Pinczewskis join her in the predominantly Jewish neighborhood of Canarsie.

The family moved at the beginning of 1960. On July 5, 1960, Helen gave birth to a son, Benjamin, who was born by C-section. In the weeks that followed, Helen suffered greatly. She developed a staph infection in the incision in her abdomen and was unable, yet again, to attend her son's *bris milah*. Her varicose veins had worsened during her pregnancy, to the degree that she could barely walk. Despite her own medical problems, what worried Helen the most were her concerns about the *Chucha*, who was in terrible pain and dying.

Despite everything else that was going on, arrangements had to be made for Solomon's upcoming Bar Mitzvah. For survivors, their child's Bar Mitzvah is a significant milestone, signifying the foiling of Hitler's plan to destroy the Jewish people. Solomon's Bar Mitzvah was made even more emotional for Helen, by his brush with Catholicism. Surviving would have been a hollow victory indeed if she didn't see her son take on his responsibility as a Jew, perpetuating the future of Judaism. Helen's staying alive was incidental. Her being involved in the creation of future generations, that was important.

So plans went ahead. Despite Helen's sadness about the *Chucha,* she booked a popular dance band, reserved the synagogue hall, and argued with caterers about the menu.

The *Torah* portion for Solomon's *Bar Mitzvah* was *Vayishlach.* Sol stood before his people and repeated the words of Genesis:11. "And God said unto him: 'I am God Almighty. Be fruitful and multiply; a nation and a company of nations shall be of thee, and kings shall come out of thy loins." Helen smiled up at her son Solomon standing straight and tall on the *bimah*, and at her younger son Benjamin, tripping on the fringes of the full-sized *tallis* wrapped around him, and knew she had done her part to comply with that instruction.

In the Rabbi's speech he talked about the "The Song of Miriam" reminding his congregants that only four biblical women were given the accolade of prophetess: Deborah, Huldah, Noadiah, and Miriam. Before Moses was born, Miriam had prophesied. "My mother will at some time bear a son who will deliver Israel." Miriam was also a symbol of joy: "And Miriam the prophetess, the sister of Aaron, took a timbrel in her hand. With timbrel and with dances Miriam sang unto them."

As Sol spoke about the revered prophetess, everyone who knew of *Bubbe* Miriam felt her presence. Even those who did not know of her felt her spirit and her energy without knowing what to attribute it to.

The guests were mainly survivors, *greeners* who looked around approvingly at the hall and the tables full of food. "Nu, Helen and David have finally made it," they said to each other. Some went on to comment about the table of guests who were clearly "goyim." Besides for the more subtle differences in their appearance, there were joyous *Mama mias*, and much praising of The Lord, at the table where Martha, Josie, and her two daughters, the *Gaon* and his wife sat. Max's widow, Anna, and her daughter, Dinah, explained to anyone who asked that those were candy store people; friends and neighbors from Bay Ridge.

The band played all the latest hit songs, and Sol and his friends took full advantage of the music. Eventually, even Helen and David succumbed to the pull of Chubby Checker.

To the delighted applause of their guests, they twisted and turned, "around and around and a up and a down." There was so much good spirit that at midnight no one wanted to go home, so they paid overtime for the band, opened a few more bottles of kosher wine, and drank toasts to Helen and David and Solomon.

"*Mazal Tov*, Solomon. Today you are a man."

In the eyes of the community Solomon did become a man that day, but since he hadn't enjoyed the usual carefree comforts of childhood, the day had a different significance for Helen. She took him aside in a quiet moment and, looking into his eyes, said, "You are more than a man. You are the proof that nothing can destroy us! Be a mensch and always remember who you come from and what your family has been through." She hugged him tightly to her. "I am alive! You are alive! Thank you, God."

Meeting his mother's gaze, Solomon resolved that his Bar Mitzvah was not a culmination but rather a beginning, and that he would try and bring some of the tenacity and resolve to his life that his parents had exhibited in theirs. His parents' history and hardships had been so deeply absorbed by him that sometimes he felt he had lived it all.

As if he had been with them in Europe, living in fear, forced to make life and death decisions.

As Sol's eyes told his mother everything she wanted to hear, Helen smiled broadly and kissed Sol on the top of his head. "Now go. Have fun. Be happy. Never forget the power of love and laughter. They can defeat any enemy!"

She went back to her guests, and Sol watched her dancing with his father as the singer crooned on about Blueberry Hill.

Sol was not yet ready to return to the party. All the intensely emotional images of the day whirled around in his mind. The cantor's evocative voice. The silky texture of the new *tallis* his mother had put around his shoulders. The sight of the large teardrops falling freely down his father's face. But what he felt most deeply was the overwhelming need not to disappoint all the people who were looking up at him standing on the *bimah*.

As his mind settled on the vision of the eternal light burning above the torah scrolls, he looked over at his mother, glowing under the compliments of her guests. In her too, that flame, the *ner tamid*, burned so strongly nothing could extinguish it.

Sol began softly to sing along with the music, "The moon stood still on Blueberry Hill."

America was his home, but a part of him would always be in Sosnowiec. He would always be aware of the dark brutality that lurks in the human soul. Yet, the example of his mother's unvanquished spirit had shown him that in the end, love and faith could prove stronger than the most intense evil the world has known.

EPILOGUE

I BEGAN MY QUEST for information with my mother.

Little by little, she would share some of the images, snippets of conversations, and emotional reactions from her life. Each of these was put into the context of a story she would share over and over again. Reduced to words, the horror of the experiences dissipated. In this way a distance could be created between the teller and the tale, so that, eventually some stories could be repeated over and over without too much pain.

In time my mother told me all she could recall of the war years. She told me about being a teenage girl without freedom or dignity and about being deported, tattooed, and marched from Buchenwald to Gross-Rosen and on to Bergen-Belsen.

The years she had spent in the insane agony of the Nazi concentration camps were an integral part of who she was. However, she could not have lived as she did with that brutal inhumanity at the forefront of her conscious mind, and mercifully most of what she endured was relegated to her subconscious.

At the end of a day of listening, I lay in bed with tears with flowing down my cheeks. I tried to understand the desperate gnawing of hunger, the anguish of thirst, and the deep humiliation of rape. I tried to understand how, amidst the agonizing terror and deprivation, there were humorous incidents that made her laugh at someone's foibles. Generous acts that made her cry at someone's goodness. I scrutinized the faded, crinkled photographs she had saved and tried to visualize her past.

She also talked with me about the early years of her marriage in post-war Germany, and her struggles to take care of a child in the frightening New World. Over and over she thanked God for her life, and repeated that *Bubbe* Miriam was the single most powerful reason for her survival. She insisted that *Bubbe* Miriam's spirit was always with her. I was not really sure what to make of that. Was she suggesting *Bubbe* Miriam took on some supernatural form? Or was it that her memories of *Bubbe* Miriam had sustained her like a glowing coal that kept alight her determination to live?

I also spoke with my father. He told me about being a Jewish boy in the anti-Semitic Polish army, and of being a young man struggling to hold on to his masculinity and humanity when the whole Nazi regime was aimed at taking both from him. He told me of his work with the partisans and how he turned down an opportunity to escape with them because he would not abandon my mother. He described the single-mindedness needed to stay alive in a concentration camp, and the horror of discovering, after he was liberated, that besides except for his brother, Max, his entire family had been annihilated.

I contacted everyone who might know anything about my parents' lives in Poland, in Germany, and their early years in Brooklyn and the Bronx. I made calls and I wrote and read letters until I was totally drained. Exhausted, I tried to process what I was hearing. As more of my mother's stories began to unfold, I was once again consumed with unanswered questions, and I went back to my sources. Still I could not understand. I tried to stretch my mind around the stories I was hearing. On the one hand, I was struggling to internalize the concept of pure evil, which I had never before contemplated so vividly, and on the other hand, I was overwhelmed by examples of individual kindness and courage that far exceeded my assumptions of what could possibly be expected from people living under such extreme circumstances. Above all, I marveled at my mother's ability to always shift her perspective, so that no matter what transpired, she always found something for which to be thankful. When at the age of seventy, she fell in the shower and broke her wrist she still found something to be grateful for. "Thank God," she said," "that it wasn't my hip."

When I asked her how she managed to maintain this positive outlook she said, "Listen, Sol, I was blind for the first three years of my life, and for ten years after that I had to wear dark glasses. Do you think that because I couldn't see the sun it wasn't up there? Of course it was. It's always there. You gotta remember that. That's what I do. Till today I always do that. To be honest with you, I gotta admit, sometimes it's very difficult, but I always try."

As I continued my research, I made voluminous notes. I wrote everything down on five by seven index cards and laid them out on the living room floor. I considered how best to organize them. By time? By place? Or perhaps by the feelings they evoked. I picked up the most recent card. It was from a school assignment written by my third cousin, ten-year-old Jennifer Stybel. Jennifer's fifth grade report was about the man and the woman she most admired. The woman she chose was my mother, Helen Pinczewski. Although she had only met my mother twice, once at her grandfather's funeral and once at a congregational Passover Seder in 1995; my mother's personality had a significant impact on Jennifer. This is what she wrote.

"I also greatly admire my grandfather's cousin Helen Pinczewski. She survived life in a concentration camp. After the Holocaust, she proceeded to the United States and made a life for herself. Although many of my relatives survived the Holocaust, it was she who instilled in me a great sense of family. She is so upbeat, has such a positive attitude, and tells great stories. I admire all this about her."

"Upbeat." Someone whose life had been as harrowing as my mother's is seen by a ten-year-old as being upbeat? Had she always been like that? Is that how she survived? Or had survival made her so joyful to be alive?

I decided I would organize my information chronologically, and patch together the quilt of my mother's life, beginning with her childhood in Poland. Maybe then I would have a picture of WHO my mother was, and HOW she survived and remained so life embracing. As to the WHY's of her life... my mind still balks at the question.

Everyting I remember about my childhood is an enigma. I was a Jewish boy going to Yeshiva with a rosary hidden in my pocket. I slept on crates in the back of a candy store, but my schoolmates thought I was rich because I had candy, egg-creams and ice cream every day. I had a mother who worked sixteen to eighteen hours a day, but was always laughing and constantly thanked God for His generosity to her. I had a strong and fearless father who loved me, but whose anger and frustration was often taken out on me in a way that made us both very afraid.

Unlike so many other Jewish immigrants of that time, I lived in a predominantly Italian Catholic neighborhood. Right next door to me lived a family who took me into their warm and loving hearts. This Italian Catholic Fusaro family generously made me one of their own and did their best to compensate for the emotional, spiritual, and recreational limitations of my life. My parents had never thought of Judaism as something to be taught to their children, so that even when we sat *shiva* for my uncle Max, I had no idea what was going on. But I was very afraid of death. Dominick Fusaro, Pop Fusaro's middle son, gave me a God I could believe in. He would come in on a sweltering hot day and say, "Heh, Helen, can I take Sol to the movies?"

"Yes please. Thank you," she's say. Unaware that the movies he took me to would be the beginning of my attachment to Catholicism.

The Mafia boss who took us under his wing was a Catholic who looked like Robert DeNiro and sounded like Marlon Brando in the movie *The Godfather*. He started off as a customer but soon became the quiet, calm source of street wisdom and control we desperately needed in that neighborhood. He took care of everything from keeping my parents solvent to seeing that they got to see Jackie Gleason. He also invited my mom and dad to go to the Copacabana to see Frank Sinatra. My mom said she would prefer to see Steve Lawrence and Edye Gorme. She wanted to hear Yiddish songs and "My Yiddisha Mama" sung by Steve Lawrence. He arranged for the front row table for their Tuesday evening off to enjoy the show.

How he knew so much about organized crime and how he had such power and commanded so much respect in those parts is a question that his help and generosity to us inclines me to leave unanswered.

APPENDEX

My Mom's Eternal Flame

Bubba Miriam Gleitman, Sosnowiecz, Poland Early 1900's

My Paternal Grandmother

Dina Pinczewski, David's Mother, Taken Bendzin, Poland, 1920's

Gleitman Family

From Left to Right, Leah, Helen, Bubba Miriam, Benjjamin Gleitman, Sosnowiecz, Poland Circa 1928 in their home.

My Maternal Grandfather

Benjamin Gleitman, Sosnowiecz, Poland Circa 1928

Helen as a young girl

My Dad

David Pinczewski, Hof, Germany, Circa 1945

Mom Post WW II

Helen Pinczewski, Hof, Germany 1946.

Mozel Tov

December 2 1945 Marriage of David Pinczewski and Helen Gleitman. Hof, Germany

Uncle Max, Hanka and Baby Dinah

Max, Hanka and Dinah Pinczewski. Hof, Germany, 1947

My Fourth Birthday Party

Solomon Pinczewski's 4th Birthday, Bronx, NY.. 11/28/1952. F
ront row, left to right AnnEllen Glatman, Solomon Pinczewski, Dinah Pinczewksi, Mark Glatman,. Back row: Alan Glatman, Simon Stybel, Hankah Pinczewski, Gloria Glatman (Mark and his brother's mother), Max Pinczewski

Graveside Yertzheit for Max Pinczewski

Dinah, Solomon and Helen Pinczewski (pregnant with Benjamin) beside Max Pinczewski's grave, Sping 1960, Beth Israel Cemetery Woodbridge, NJ

Mom visiting Uncle's Max Grave

Helen Pinczewsi visiting her brother-in-law Max's grave just before Roshashannah , Circa 1962

Dad's Kever Avot for Uncle Max

David Pinczewsi visiting his brother, Max's grave just before Roshashannah , Circa 1962

Dad in front of the Candy Store

David Pinczewski 1404 86th Street, Brooklyn, New York, late 1950's

Pop Fusaro, Mom and Me behind the candy Store.

Behind 1404 86th , Brooklyn New York. Circa 1957

Me and Dad Behind the Candy Store

David and Solomon Pinczewski behind 1404 86th Street, Brooklyn, NY 1959

Helen Pinczewski in Candy Store

Helen Pinczewski in Candy Store with The Gaon behind her with his arm around her shoulder

My Dad and Me in Front of the 19th Hole

David Pinczewsiki, Solomon Pinczewski circa, January/February 1960, Brooklyn, New York, Corner of 14th avenue and 86th Street.

Mom with visible tatoo and Dad at My Wedding

Helen and David Pinczewzki at Solomon's marriage to Ellen Cooper, Lynbrook, NY 12/29/1974

Mom and Dad's 50th Temple Celebration

Helen and David Pinczewsli at B'nai Emet Synagogue Congregates Golden Anniversary celebration Del Ray Beach, FL December 1995.

Mom and Dad's 50th Wedding Anniversary

Helen and David Pinczewski's 50th Anniversary. Del Ray Beach, FL 12/2/1995.
From Left to Right Jessica, Solomon, Ellen, Jacquiline, Helen, David, Kathy Graff, Benjamin

Helen Looking at her two sons, who were her pride and joy!

June 2005, at Helen's great niece, Marni Goldman's wedding to Greg Rosenzweig in Santa Monica, CA. Left to Right - Solomon, Helen and Benjamin Pinczewski.

Listen to the radio broadcast: https://soundcloud.com/user-216785693-138462459/sol-on-weva-with-zuee-schooler-1962-1
View the album: https://windows-on-the-world.smugmug.com/Family/Sols-Book/n-PHk3b3/

Made in the USA
San Bernardino, CA
06 July 2020